SEMINAR STUDIES IN HISTORY

Editor: Patrick Richardson

KING JOHN AND
MAGNA CARTA

SEMINAR STUDIES IN HISTORY

Editor: Patrick Richardson

A full list of titles in this
series will be found on the
back cover of this book

SEMINAR STUDIES IN HISTORY

KING JOHN AND MAGNA CARTA

J. A. P. Jones

LONGMAN

LONGMAN GROUP LIMITED
London

ASSOCIATED COMPANIES, BRANCHES AND
REPRESENTATIVES THROUGHOUT THE WORLD

First published 1971

ISBN 0 582 31463 1

DA208
.J65

PRINTED IN GREAT BRITAIN BY
WESTERN PRINTING SERVICES LTD, BRISTOL

Contents

Part Four · The Great Charter 1215

Part Five · Documents

Introduction to the Series

The seminar method of teaching is being used increasingly. It is a way of learning in smaller groups through discussion, designed both to get away from and to supplement the basic lecture techniques. To be successful, the members of a seminar must be informed—or else, in the unkind phrase of a cynic—it can be a 'pooling of ignorance'. The chapter in the textbook of English or European history by its nature cannot provide material in this depth, but at the same time the full academic work may be too long and perhaps too advanced.

For this reason we have invited practising teachers to contribute short studies on specialised aspects of British and European history with these special needs in mind.

For this series the authors have been asked to provide, in addition to their basic analysis, a full selection of documentary material of all kinds and an up-to-date and comprehensive bibliography. Both these sections are referred to in the text, but it is hoped that they will prove to be valuable teaching and learning aids in themselves.

Note on the System of References:

A bold number in round brackets (**5**) in the text refers the reader to the corresponding entry in the Bibliography section at the end of the book.

A bold number in square brackets, preceded by 'doc.' [**docs 6, 8**] refers the reader to the corresponding items in the section of Documents, which follows the main text.

PATRICK RICHARDSON
General Editor

Acknowledgements

We are grateful to the following for permission to reproduce copyright material:

Clarendon Press, Oxford for short extracts from *The Northerners; A Study in the Reign of King John* by J. C. Holt, 1961; Cambridge University Press for extracts from *Magna Carta* by J. C. Holt; Thomas Nelson and Sons Limited for extracts from *Selected Letters of Pope Innocent III* edited by C. R. Cheney and W. H. Semple; Eyre and Spottiswoode (Publishers) Limited and Oxford University Press Inc. for extracts from *English Historical Documents, Volume II*.

The cover photograph of an effigy of King John at Worcester Cathedral is by courtesy of Professor Lawrence Stone.

Preface

Many students have doubted the value and relevance of medieval history: their doubts can be answered by sympathetic reference to the reign of King John. Not only is there a modern ring about the 'revolutionary situation' created by the barons of Magna Carta in 1215, but also, in placing the king beneath the law, Magna Carta tackled the thorny, and again modern, problem of the relationship between society and authority. It must be emphasised, however, that thirteenth-century political, social and legal forms were totally different from our own, an essentially ecclesiastic and legalistic structure where political relationships were formed amid slow communications and powerful rumours. Much of the modern interpretation of Magna Carta is no more than a continuation of the 'myth' which built up around the Charter in the thirteenth century; it is, therefore, important to uncover the myth by reference to the events which produced it. The value and relevance of the reign of King John lie as much in its contrast as in its similarity with our own day.

For the student of history, moreover, medieval England offers great reward in terms of method: the conflict of fascinating and prejudiced contemporary opinion and more objective but limited recorded evidence presents a stimulating challenge, which can often be resolved only by careful and imaginative reconstruction. I became aware of this initially through the teaching of C. R. Cheney, Professor of Medieval History at Cambridge, to whom I am also indebted for advice and generosity, without which this book could not have been written. For its faults, of course, he is in no way responsible. In addition my thanks are due to T. J. Nicholls for his help with the maps, and to Mrs J. M. Brown, whose interest and care in typing the manuscript helped to make the writing of it such a pleasure.

Part One

THE
BACKGROUND

1 The Angevins to 1204

THE ANGEVIN SYSTEM

After the civil war in England between King Stephen and the Empress Matilda, it was Matilda's son, Henry, who came to the throne in 1154 and started the Angevin dynasty. According to Gerald the Welshman, Henry II

> not only brought strong peace with the aid of God's grace to his hereditary dominions, but also triumphed victoriously in remote and foreign lands, a thing of which none of his predecessors since the coming of the Normans, not even the English kings, had proved capable. . . . Furthermore he vigorously extended his dominions overseas in Gaul and Aquitaine; to Anjou, Maine and Touraine which he inherited from his father, and Poitou and the whole of Gascony as far as the Pyrenees, which had fallen to his lot by marriage, he added Auvergne, Berri and Gisors, together with the Vexin which had formerly been taken from Normandy (**15, p. 381**).

Henry's father, Geoffrey of Anjou, had added Normandy to his lands in 1144 and done homage to Louis VII of France for the duchy in 1149. On Geoffrey's death in 1151 Henry received all his father's lands, as well as his mother's title to England. In 1153 he sailed to England and, after the death of Stephen's son, Eustace of Boulogne, signed the Treaty of Winchester by which he was to become Stephen's heir. In the previous year, moreover, he had acquired the whole of Aquitaine by his marriage to Eleanor, who had been divorced three months earlier by Louis VII. Thus by 1154 when Stephen died the Angevin 'Empire' had been created: of his thirty-five years as King of England, Henry spent over twenty in his continental possessions, and his son Richard was absent on crusade for most of his ten-year reign. Hence, English government had to be reformed to operate efficiently in the king's absence.

The main cog in the Angevin machine was the justiciar, the king's *alter ego* who had sole direction of government affairs in the king's absence and could issue chancery writs in his own name. He was also Chairman of the Bench, the judicial court permanent at Westminster and especially useful when the king himself, with his own personal court, *coram rege*, was out of the country. He also supervised the chancery and exchequer clerks, the growing professional bureaucracy on which so much of Henry II's legal and judicial reforms relied. Much has already been written about these reforms (**1, 12, 40, 41**): the procedure of the Grand and Possessory Assizes was initiated by writs purchased from the king's chancery: once a certain writ was purchased, the procedure followed a set pattern and could not be altered, thus operating largely independent of personalities. The possession of land was now protected by the king's justice; any disputes about it must be conducted in the king's court, either *coram rege* or the bench, or by one of the itinerant justices in eyre. Henry's reign also instituted a more widespread use of the jury, not as judges of fact, but rather as witnesses, summoned by royal officials to give evidence. This judicial and legal machinery, continued throughout the thirteenth century, gave rise to the Common Law, the use of the king's court for all cases for all men during the reign of Edward I. Magna Carta did not object to it on behalf of a selfish feudal baronage; rather did it want it administered more efficiently, and more fairly.

Similarly Henry's local government had to operate in his absence. He tried initially to appoint royal favourites, men he could trust, as sheriffs, but complaints of financial oppression led him in 1170 to conduct the Inquest of Sheriffs: itinerant justices were sent to each shire to inquire into the behaviour of sheriffs, foresters and other royal baronial officials, and to concentrate especially on financial exactions. As a result of the inquiry many sheriffs were removed and replaced by men even closer to the king's service, especially in the Exchequer. The sheriff, in fact, was the local official who made the Angevin financial and judicial systems work, collecting taxes, handling writs, assembling amercements, preparing for the justices in assize and so on. It was in the shire court, too, that all men took the oath of allegiance to the king, requested by the Assize of Northampton of 1176. The oath was particularly important because military service to the king rested on the feudal relationship of lord and vassal. To ensure the efficient working of this service Henry conducted the *Cartae Baronum* in 1166: each tenant in chief had to supply to the king the amount of service, in knight's fees, he owed in return for his land. Further, the Assize of Arms of 1181 implied the use of a permanently armed and ready, almost professional, army.

Financial administration, too, was organised to function efficiently without the king: the Exchequer had grown apart from the House-hold which followed the ambulatory king's court, and the Treasurer was given a duplicate Great Seal to authorise financial documents. The workings of the Exchequer became stereotyped, following the procedures of receipt, account, and audit described in the *Dialogue* (**28**), although still using the primitive abacus and tallies for the accounts. Procedure was slow, but organised and efficient. Moreover, in the collection of revenue, Henry, like John, was ruthless: as Barlow has said:

> He extracted the maximum gain from his feudal rights; he made royal justice more profitable; and he accepted greedily all those 'fines', offerings and bribes, without which he would grant no favour. Among feudal rights, wardship (especially of the vacant bishoprics) remained the most lucrative and marriage the most politically valuable. Baronial reliefs were commonly at £100 or 100 marks, but they were still at the will of the king, and Henry used his discretion so as to punish his enemies and reward his friends (**1,** p. 311).

This might easily have been said, in criticism, of King John. Indeed it is of the utmost importance, to emphasise the continuity of the Angevin system: the loss of Normandy in 1204 meant that John spent nearly all his reign in England, with the result that the machine, built to function in the king's absence, was now used with even greater efficiency by a resident king, anxious to recover his lost lands. The difference between John and Henry II was largely one of degree: and the barons in John's reign rarely had the safety valve of either the king's absence or the repeated rebellions of his sons in which to work off their grievances.

Typical of Angevin administration was Hubert Walter, the chancellor and justiciar of Richard I and Archbishop of Canterbury until 1205. Professor Cheney has emphasised Hubert's very personal contribution to the running of Richard's government from 1193 to 1198 (**9**). He had, first of all, to keep England safe for Richard during the revolt of Prince John in 1193; to do so he besieged Marlborough castle himself, summoned a council of nobles and bishops to disseise John of all the land he held in England and to attack all the castles which John's supporters held. Finally he summoned a clerical assembly at Westminster to excommunicate John if he still refused to relent. Moreover, he took important measures to keep the peace during the next five years: in 1194 he issued comprehensive instructions or 'articles' to the justices in eyre, in 1195 he ordered all men over fifteen years of age to take an oath to keep the peace and in 1197 summoned the great men of the realm to Oxford to supply military aid for the king's wars. His most telling contribution, however, was probably in judicial and administrative reform. He instituted that all final concords in judicial cases be preserved in triplicate, the third part being kept for reference by the treasurer, and he also began the enrolment of all Chancery letters and documents in 1200, material again useful for reference. Walter was typical of the professional clerical administrator who made the Angevin machine more efficient. It was the barons who equated this efficiency with tyranny.

KING JOHN

John was the youngest son of Henry II and succeeded his brother Richard in 1199. There was, however, a rival candidate to the throne, Arthur, the son of Geoffrey, John's elder brother. Richard's successor, therefore, could be either his youngest brother or his nephew. Now the laws of inheritance were not fixed: Glanville, for instance, recognised the claims of the nephew, while the *Tres Ancien Coutumier*, the customary law of Normandy, preferred the claim of the younger son. The *Histoire de Guillaume de Maréchal* reveals a conversation between Hubert Walter and the Marshal about the succession: the Archbishop supports Arthur, the Marshal supports John (**11**). Both John and Arthur were well supported among the barons, the former being favoured largely by Anglo-Normans while the latter could count on the support of Angevins, Poitevins and of course, Bretons, as well as his alliance with Philip Augustus, the powerful king of France. John's first task was therefore, through William Marshal, to summon the English baronage to Northampton to discuss grievances and to send Eustace de Vesci to see his father-in-law, King William of Scotland. John then briefly visited England to be crowned at Westminster by Walter, before returning to Normandy to tackle the alliance of Arthur and Philip; after long discussions the Treaty of le Goulet was signed with Philip by which John was recognised as Richard's heir and Arthur was to hold Brittany as his vassal. John, however, was to recognise Philip's overlordship for all his continental possessions, a clause which was to be of crucial importance in the following years. Finally the treaty was cemented by the marriage of John's niece, Blanche, to Philip's son, Louis, and John's payment of 20,000 marks to Philip. For the next two years an uneasy peace was maintained between John and Philip, but during this time John fell foul of the family of Lusignan, important Poitevin barons. In 1199 he had recognised Hugh of Lusignan's claim to La Marche, a county disputed between Hugh and Ademar of Angoulême. In the following year, however, John became attracted to Isabella of Angoulême, Ademar's daughter who was already betrothed to Hugh of Lusignan, and married her; moreover, he himself took over the administration of La Marche in defiance of the Lusignan claims. This was a double blow to Hugh who appealed to John's overlord, Philip, for a trial; Philip in turn summoned John to his feudal court but John refused to attend. He was therefore declared a contumacious vassal and his lands confiscated. Powicke has told in detail the story of the loss of Normandy (**46**): both John and Philip realised the value of Arthur, who was now in rebellion with his Bretons and besieging Eleanor at Mirabeau, in company with the rebel barons of Lusignan. John's quick march to Mirabeau from Le Mans and his capture of Arthur and the Lusignans rank as his one real military success. Yet it was his failure as a military leader which caused the eventual loss of Normandy: only Hubert de Burgh at Chinon, Gerard D'Athée at Loches and Roger de Lacy at Chateau-Gaillard held out for John against the joint advance of Philip from the east and William des Roches, the seneschal of Anjou and Touraine, from the south. The usual attitude of the Norman baronage was that of Robert FitzWalter and Saer de Quenci, who surrendered Vaudreuil, the crucial Seine fortress, without a fight.

The final fate of Arthur has long been a subject for speculation among historians. Powicke has inclined towards the view of the Margam chronicler, that John murdered Arthur in a drunken rage at Rouen in 1203 and threw the body, tied to a stone, into the Seine. Certainly John was at Rouen at Easter 1203, and the Margam chronicler was usually well informed by William de Braose, John's constant companion during 1203–4 (**46,** pp. 316–21). It is even more difficult to assess whether Philip heard of Arthur's death before 1204 and used it as a reason for a second trial and condemnation of John; rumours of murder were certainly rife among the Breton and Angevin baronage, though it is impossible to estimate their effect. In addition, many of Arthur's colleagues at Mirabeau were captured by John and the Margam Annals believe that twenty-two were starved to death at Corfe castle, while Arthur's sister appears to have been imprisoned at Bristol until 1241 when she died. The rumours of tyranny that surrounded the murder of Arthur, and the effects on John and England of the loss of Normandy become recurrent themes during the reign of King John. His insistent attempts to recover Normandy and the mutual distrust existing between him and his barons, together with several other factors like his conflict with the Church, led John into baronial conspiracy and civil war by 1215.

Part Two

DESCRIPTIVE
NARRATIVE
1204–15

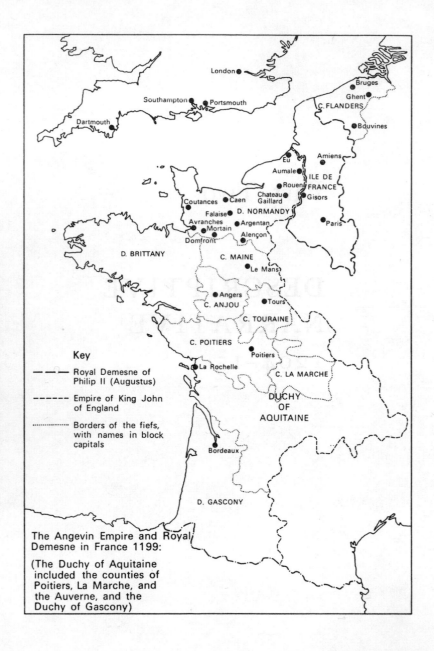

London●

Southampton● ●Portsmouth

Dartmouth●

●Bruges
●Ghent
C. FLANDERS

●Bouvines

Eu●
Aumale● Amiens

Coutances● ●Caen
Falaise●
Avranches● ●Argentan
●Mortain
Domfront● Alençon●

●Rouen ILE DE FRANCE
Chateau Gisors●
Gaillard

D. NORMANDY

●Paris

D. BRITTANY

C. MAINE
●Le Mans

●Angers ●Tours
C. ANJOU
C. TOURAINE

C. POITIERS

La Rochelle● ●Poitiers
C. LA MARCHE

DUCHY OF AQUITAINE

●Bordeaux

D. GASCONY

Key

— — — Royal Demesne of
Philip II (Augustus)

- - - - - Empire of King John
of England

············· Borders of the fiefs,
with names in block
capitals

The Angevin Empire and Royal
Demesne in France 1199:

(The Duchy of Aquitaine
included the counties of
Poitiers, La Marche, and
the Auverne, and the
Duchy of Gascony)

2 John's Efforts to Recover Normandy, 1204–14

Professor Holt summarises the key problem that King John faced throughout his reign thus:

> John's most decisive action was not that he lost Normandy, the Touraine, and the old Angevin influence in the Midi, but that for ten furious years he devoted all his attention to regaining what he had lost. He was a true son of Eleanor of Aquitaine. To argue that he should have accepted the decision of 1204 is unrealistic. Not even his son, Henry III, was prepeared to abandon the old Angevin claims until 1259, and he only did so then under the pressure of events in England. Thus, in the chronology of John's reign, 1204, not 1199, is the crucial date (**23,** p. 144).

In 1205 both John and Philip Augustus were making detailed preparations, the one to recover the lands he had lost, the other to secure his grip on them. Philip crossed the Loire and took Chinon and Loches from their castellans Hubert de Burgh and Gerard D'Athée; he also captured John's seneschal in Poitou, Robert of Thornham. John's own support rested largely on Savary de Mauléon, a former rebel imprisoned by John in 1202 but by 1205 a trusted ally, who strove to keep the allegiance of the Poitevin barons and important fortresses like La Rochelle and Niort. John had originally planned an expedition to recover his lost territory in 1205, but was dissuaded by William the Marshal and other notables since his preparations were not complete; throughout 1205 therefore, John was aiming at finishing the work for a prompt start in the spring of the following year. On 27 April 1205 the bishop of Norwich was ordered to send ships from East Anglia to Portsmouth 'on the king's business', while in the West Country William de Marisco and John de la Warre were given 100 marks to spend on 'the hiring of ships'.

Naval historians appear to agree that there was a general impressment in the spring of 1205, evidence for which comes not only from the Pipe Roll of that year, but also from Coggeshall, who describes the concentration of ships at Dartmouth under Geoffrey, the king's illegitimate son. It seems from the evidence, in fact, that the king was using three points of embarkation, Dartmouth, Portsmouth and Southampton: perhaps he intended to keep Philip guessing at which point on the Continent he would aim. Preparations were also made for provisioning the fleet: on 29 March a writ to the sheriff of Oxford ordered 300 bacons to be taken to Southampton and similar writs went to the sheriffs of Surrey and Northamptonshire. Finally, the Pipe Roll reveals a muster of land forces at Northampton on 22 May, with fines for those who failed to attend. It is clear that such thorough preparation affected a large part of the country; similarly detailed planning for later expeditions in 1213 and 1214, as well as other expeditions to Wales, Ireland and Scotland, were to arouse hostility against the king's use of English resources overseas.

For John the key to the successful recovery of Normandy was the loyalty of the Poitevin and Norman baronage; he had been taught a severe lesson by the loss of the strategically placed fortress of Vaudreuil in 1203 through the weakness of Saer de Quenci and Robert FitzWalter, who surrendered the castle to Philip, bringing on themselves charges of bribery and cowardice from the chroniclers. It was always a source of weakness to John that many of his leading notables possessed land in both England and Normandy, and this weakness was emphasised in two important cases in 1205 and 1206. William Marshal was one of the greatest barons in England: as well as the shires of Gloucester and Sussex he had the custody of the royal castle of Cardigan and estates throughout England and Wales. But in addition he held lands in Normandy, for which he performed liege homage to Philip Augustus, so that in 1205 he had to refuse to accompany John's expedition. Ralph of Exoudun was Count of Eu and one of the most prominent barons in Poitou; he also possessed lands in Normandy and England for which he had done homage to John in 1202, and his support was vital if John was to succeed in 1206. Philip realised this and early in that year sent a messenger to Ralph to bargain with him: he offered Ralph the whole of Poitou for five years, together with £4,000 Parisienne a year and 100 knights and 1,000 foot soldiers for three months every year. In return Ralph was to defend Poitou against Philip's enemies, 'for the land of Poitou is so distant and far that he cannot have communication with it as with the rest of his land', and also to hand over his lands in Normandy to Philip as security [**doc. 5**]. Perhaps Philip believed that John's expedition would aim directly at Normandy so that a loyal and powerful baron would give him security in Poitou. The case does, however, indicate the decisive value of the local baronage to both Philip and John, which can be further illustrated by the chequered career of Savary de Mauleon (**7**). The loyalty of these men was usually dictated by advantage, a grant of land, a money fief or military protection from a powerful overlord; John had therefore to recover the prestige lost in 1204 by proving his military ability and might in his new venture.

On 26 May 1206 he set sail. The chroniclers are of little help in our attempts to follow the course of his expedition: for example, only the Bury Chronicler has the correct date of embarkation, while only Walter of Coventry is shrewd enough to note the purpose of the expedition: 'The king went to Poitou for the recovery of his lost lands and captured a few castles.' The central action of the expedition was the siege of Mons Alba, and in his description of this Wendover builds up the dramatic content of his work with little thought for accuracy: after showing how the whole military nobility of Gascony was hostile to John, he describes the siege and capture of Mons Alba, 'that which Charlemagne could not subjugate even after a seven year siege'. Worcester is the only other annalist to give any detail: he notes the capture of the seneschal of the King of Spain as well as 120 knights and 200 serjeants. None of the chroniclers gives us any more than this basic story.

The official records, on the other hand, are a little more useful. The Pipe Roll for 1205 records the expenses of fortifying the Channel Islands in the spring and of raising a new fleet in October. The records also reveal why John preferred to strike at Normandy from Poitou rather than make a direct frontal attack: he believed in the loyal Angevin party of Poitevins under Savary de Mauléon and also in the loyalty of several of the stronger towns like Bordeaux and La Rochelle, which had important trading connections with England. John therefore thought he could strike north into Normandy more easily from the security of a base in Poitou. Moreover, as Philip's letter to the Count of Eu indicated, he had great difficulty himself in controlling the independent barons of the south-west because of the great distance from Paris. Yet there was another, more important,

13

reason for attacking Poitou in 1206: not only had Blanche, the daughter of Alfonso VIII of Castile, married Prince Louis, dauphin of France, but in addition Alfonso himself, as a son-in-law of Henry I of England, claimed Gascony in his own right. Many Gascon nobles, hating Angevin overlordship, had paid homage to Alfonso and he had moved many knights into Poitou. We learn from the Patent Rolls that many Spaniards were shipped to England after the capture of Mons Alba, while the Pipe Roll for 1213 records detailed accounts for the maintenance of Spanish prisoners over the previous seven years. Moreover, the official records trace accurately John's route after the capture of Mons Alba in August; as Philip declined to come into Poitou, John marched north, crossed the Loire into Normandy and took Angers on 6 September. The next month witnessed an ineffectual campaign before a two-year truce was signed with Philip on 13 October, but the truce settled nothing: John relinquished none of his claims to Normandy but promised not to enter the duchy for two years, each king meanwhile retaining the allegiance of those barons who had fought for him during the preceding months. There is then a gap in the information until 26 October on which, the Patent Rolls reveal, John set sail for Portsmouth.

Many historians have condemned John for his failure to recapture Normandy in 1206, yet when the evidence is so bare it is difficult to get a complete picture: supplies may have failed or the Norman barons may have refused to support John, preferring the overlordship of Philip as many did in 1204. On the credit side, John was at least better established in Poitou, secure from the danger of Castile and with a suitable base for later expeditions to Normandy. Moreover, there had been little financial pressure on the barons for the expedition since the bulk of the money, £5,170, was gained from the vacancy of the see of Canterbury, while the shipping expenses came out of the farms of Reginald of Cornhill, sheriff of Kent, and William of Wrotham, the director of the ports. It was the later expedition to Poitou and the scutages for Irish and Welsh campaigns that aroused baronial hostility towards John's military ambitions. On the other hand, the king had failed again in Normandy, and, though he obviously planned to return, his failure would certainly not arouse the confidence of the local barons in the power of his overlordship.

In the year after this expedition John turned his attention to wider issues of foreign policy, though the recovery of Normandy was still his chief aim. The chroniclers give little evidence of the visit of John's nephew Otto in that year, apart from a brief account of their meeting at the house of Abbot Samson of Bury recorded by Matthew Paris. Otto was the son of John's elder sister Matilda, who had married Henry the Lion, the head of the German house of Welf and the rival to the reigning Hohenstaufen emperor, Henry VI. When Henry died in 1199 he left his young son Frederick in the care of Innocent III and, since he was still a minor, a struggle ensued for control of Germany between Otto the Welf and Philip of Swabia. In 1206 Otto had lost valuable support in the Rhineland, partly as a result of an alliance between Philip of Swabia and Philip Augustus of France. Therefore both Otto and John were anxious to break Philip's power in France, so that the one would find it easier to recover Normandy and the other would have less opposition to his succession to the Empire. Hence it was more than family connection which brought Otto to England in 1207; according to the Pipe Rolls, moreover, he was given by John a payment of 6,000 marks 'as our gift'. It could well be, in addition, that the idea for a two-pronged attack on Normandy and France, with Otto and the princes of the Low Countries attacking from the north-east, and John himself leading an army from Poitou in the south-west, was born at their meeting at Bury.

Certainly Otto's visit stimulated John into a determined search for continental allies, for Henry, archdeacon of Stafford, returned to Germany with Otto in 1208 and Henry, the Count Palatine and Otto's brother, came to England the following year to be given an annual pension of 1,000 marks by John, obviously a retaining fee for future service. In 1208 John held discussions with Alfonso IX of Leon in an attempt to strengthen his southern frontier against the pretensions of Castile, while the Mise Rolls reveal that in the following two years many knights went over to Poitou to defend the royal interest under Robert of Thornham and Geoffrey de Neville. Although the historian must beware of attaching too much significance to such movements, common in unstable political conditions, they do reveal that John was still developing his plans for the recovery of Normandy throughout these years. These plans became even more vital when in 1209 both John and Otto were excommunicated by the pope, who now became virtually an ally of Philip Augustus; they had, however, to be postponed until 1212 because of rebellions in Ireland and Wales, a conspiracy in the north and the pressure of the papal interdict on England.

In 1212 Otto was in Italy trying to reach an agreement with the pope over his claims to the Empire, and from Tuscany he sent messengers to John to confirm their alliance; in May John replied by sending an important embassy under Saer de Quenci, earl of Winchester, and Walter de Gray, the chancellor. Their alliance was now extremely important to both, for, not only was the pope supporting the claims of Frederick II against Otto, but in addition, with England still under the interdict and its king excommunicated, there were rumours that the pope had deposed John and was encouraging Philip Augustus to invade England and remove John from the throne. John therefore needed further allies in the Low Countries and was particularly fortunate to get the support of Renaud d'Ammartin, the count of Boulogne. Renaud had been a vassal and ally of Philip, cementing his alliance by a marriage of his daughter to the king's son in 1210; in the following year, however, he deserted Philip, who then captured his castles, forcing Renaud to flee to Otto for aid. In 1212 he came to England and in return for a money fief of £300 a year and the promise of reinstatement in his lands he did homage to John and gave him hostages including his wife and two sons. John also bribed the duke of Limburg and the count of Bar by restoring their fiefs in return for their homage, while Count William of Holland stated in a letter: 'I have promised King John that if foreigners attack England I will come to England with all my force at the expense of the king, and will only depart if my own land is being attacked.'

At this time it appears that John was quite afraid of an invasion by Philip or by his son Louis, since it was thought that Philip had allies among certain Welsh princes and English barons [**doc. 11**]. However, John's submission to the pope in May 1213 and the end of the interdict by his surrender of the kingdom to Innocent robbed Philip of the support of the Church. Further, John now began to assume the offensive again by mobilising his army at Barham Down in March 1213 and his navy at Portsmouth, and conducting several lightning raids on French shipping in the Seine and at Dieppe. On 28 May a fleet of 500 ships with 700 English and Flemish knights under William of Salisbury arrived in Flanders in response to an appeal from Count Ferrand for help. Ferrand had been attacked by Philip Augustus who, aware of the strategic value of the Low Countries, had probably heard of John's search for allies there. While Philip's army was besieging Ghent, the English expeditionary force routed the French fleet at Damme; it was only the refusal of service by some of his barons that prevented John from following up this success by his planned two-pronged attack on France and Normandy.

He eventually managed to set sail for Poitou in February 1214. Thorough preparations had been made during the previous year, similar to those made in 1205; ships had been refitted—some with mangers for the horses—naval stores had been collected from Gloucester, Southampton and even London, and the royal war chest, money from the castle treasuries at Bristol and Corfe, was put on board. All this was financed not only from the highest scutage of the reign, 3 marks per knight's fee, but also from a tallage on the royal demesne and monastic houses. Finally John's continental allies were ready: Savary de Mauléon, having come into his inheritance in Poitou, was now a loyal vassal and helped to secure the allegiance of other Poitevin nobles, while Otto and the princes of the Low Countries were approaching France from the north-east. John's fleet reached La Rochelle on 15 February and thereafter it is possible to trace his movements quite accurately from the orders issued by his itinerant Chancery and one or two progress reports which he sent to England.

At the beginning he met little resistance: twenty-six castles were surrendered to him immediately, for, as Viscount Guy of Limoges wrote to Philip Augustus, 'I could not resist him or await your help . . . these things I tell you so that you may know that for the future you may not rely on me' (**41,** p. 466). John marched east to Limoges, south to secure Aquitaine and then north into Normandy at Angers, the whole area being secured by the great diplomatic success of the marriage of his daughter Joan to Hugh le Brun, count of La Marche, a member of the powerful Lusignan family with whom John had quarrelled in 1201. In 1206 John had got no further into Normandy than Angers, and now again at the siege of La Roche aux Moines he was opposed by Prince Louis, the Dauphin, who had been left by his father in Normandy with just 800 knights while Philip himself had gone to face the emperor in the north-east. John, however, fled from La Roche aux Moines back to La Rochelle, probably because he suspected the loyalty of the Poitevins in his army. Coggeshall reports that John's failure was caused by the duplicity of Aimery, count of Thouars, who eventually went over to

Philip Augustus. This can be corroborated by an earlier letter from Aimery to the count of Eu suggesting an alliance against Philip since John's overlordship was of such little protective value. Clearly Philip was seen as the more powerful overlord.

In July John wrote home asking for reinforcements, especially from those of the barons who had refused to serve overseas earlier in the year; in the same letter he stated that all was going well in Poitou, but clearly it was not, for in the following month Philip, now secure on his southern flank, defeated Otto at Bouvines. John's original plan, as Poole has shown (**41**) was good, but once John failed to impose sufficient pressure on Normandy from the south, Philip could devote all his attention to the more serious threat from the north. It was the cavalry ability of the French knights, coupled with the treachery of the duke of Brabant, which enabled Philip to gain a decisive victory, in which only the earl of Salisbury and Renaud d'Ammartin put up any serious resistance.

Victory for Philip was complete over both invading armies, so that on 18 September John, still at La Rochelle, signed a truce with Philip to last until 1220; it is unlikely that this was in response to Innocent III's letter of 22 April asking for peace for a crusade, for John was decisively beaten. Coggeshall records in fact that John paid Philip 60,000 marks for the treaty, but there is no other evidence to confirm this and Coggeshall may be confusing it with the 66,000 marks paid by John to Philip in 1216. Thus, John's prestige was again lowered, his treasury was reduced, his continental allies were lost and his standing as a military leader and feudal overlord lowered in the eyes of the English baronage. As Professor Holt has written, 'the road from Bouvines to Runnymeade was direct, short, and unavoidable' (**23,** p. 100). The major effect of this long series of continental alliances and wars was the hostility it aroused among the barons, and it is to them that we must now turn.

3 John's Relations with his Barons, 1204–13

EARLY BARONIAL UNREST

Under the year 1215 Ralph of Coggeshall states that, 'the Barons of England made a "diffidatio" against their king and renounced the homage they had made to him . . . such a great terror besieged the king that he never left Windsor'. He adds that after the capture of London in May many other barons joined the rebels, including the knights or subtenants of those few earls who remained loyal to the king [**doc. 17**]. Wendover records the names of the principal barons who met at Stamford at Easter of the same year while three sources actually list the twenty-five barons who were to enforce the charter by the terms of the security clause [**docs 18, 19**]. It is important to seek the identity of these individuals, to examine their grievances and to discuss the reasons for their unification against the king. Essentially they distrusted the Angevin system of government, they desired a return to the good old days before 1154; that is why they raised up the laws of Edward the Confessor and Henry I as their standards of liberty. Painter indeed places much of the blame on Richard I, whose solution to the problems of government had been to 'wage war on his external enemies and to pay the costs by wringing every cent possible out of the people of his domain. His financial exactions were by the standard of his day utterly outrageous' (**37,** p. 18). Further, Richard was succeeded by a king permanently resident in England after 1204 and determined to stretch the Angevin machine to its limit in his attempts to make good his loss of that year; in addition, whereas Richard maintained baronial loyalty through his military prowess, John possessed no such compensating virtue. As we have already seen, he lacked completely the kingly attribute of being a leader in war: the baronial renunciation of homage in 1215 was partly the result of his weak overlordship.

At the beginning of his reign the king was easily the most powerful man in England: as well as his demesne land he held the earldom of Gloucester and in addition fifteen baronies which had escheated to the Crown, comprising 1,400 knight's fees and twelve powerful castles. Although it is impossible to assess the wealth of all the chief barons in similar terms, the most powerful were clearly the seven or eight great earls. Ranulf, earl of Chester, who controlled much of North Wales, Lancashire and the Midlands and was probably the largest landholder in England after the Church, remained loyal to John throughout the reign. So too did Robert de Beaumont, earl of Leicester, Constance, countess of Richmond, William, earl of Arundel, William de Warrenne, earl of Surrey, and Geoffrey FitzPeter, the earl of Essex who was the king's justiciar until his death in 1213. Moreover, several powerful barons quarrelled with John during his reign but remained loyal during the crisis of 1215–16; these include William de Redvers, earl of Devon, who maintained the loyalty of a large part of the West Country, and the great Earl Marshal who had extensive territory across Ireland, Wales and Normandy and who was one of the reasons for John's successful accession to the throne (**11**). Thus many of the most powerful men in the realm did not join the baronial opposition to John. The reasons for this are varied: some like Ranulf of Chester and William Redvers remained loyal because the king continued to satisfy their rapacious demands for land; others, like Geoffrey FitzPeter, continued as important administrators or justices, benefiting by royal patronage and office; others still maintained their loyalty, even if only temporarily, because they needed royal support in important lawsuits or saw the chance of military glory at the head of the king's army. Such men were Roger Bigod, earl of Norfolk, and William, earl of Salisbury, the king's half-brother. Thus loyalty was built basically on royal patronage and favour, and John could use this particularly to place 'new men' in key offices in government (**23,** ch. 12), such men as Robert de Vieupont who was advanced by John from a household sergeant to a great northern landholder and Brian de Lisle who, from a royal knight, became one of the great administrators of the north. John also used his patronage to ensure the loyalty of mercenary leaders whom he intruded into English local government, men like Gerard D'Athée and Philip Mark.

If possession of office and favour could ensure the loyalty of the 'king's friends', then deprivation and loss of these could arouse the hostility of his opponents; as Holt has shown.

20

By and large they were the 'outs' excluded from the spoils of office, despite a family tradition of service to the Crown in many cases, despite the earlier administrative experience which some of them enjoyed and despite the expectancy of office which their social position gave them. In addition many of them had personal wrongs, grievances and problems to set right. . . . Theirs was a rebellion of the aggrieved, of the failures; a protest against the quasi-monopoly of office by the king and his friends (**23,** pp. 33-4).

This can be well illustrated by the careers of three rebels, Robert de Ros, Robert FitzWalter and Saer de Quenci, earl of Winchester, all of whom were members of the Twenty-Five in 1215. Robert de Ros was one of the king's friends, who accompanied John to Ireland in 1210 and acted as one of the baronial guarantors of John's agreement with Langton in 1213. He was, moreover, a son-in-law of the king of Scotland and often employed by John in embassies to Scotland. But in 1196 and again in 1207 he allowed two royal prisoners, both his own tenants, to escape from his custody for which he had to pay 150 marks in amercements, and in 1205 he was disseised of his lands temporarily by the king, merely on suspicion. He joined the rebels in 1215, probably after the fall of London. Robert FitzWalter and Saer de Quenci had both been high in the royal favour before 1203: both had married well to the sisters of earls and both were considered loyal enough to be given joint command of Vaudreuil, a key fortress in the defence of Rouen, in John's plans for the defence of Normandy in 1203. Yet they surrendered Vaudreuil to Philip Augustus with very little resistance and as a result aroused the king's suspicion. When Earl Robert of Leicester died in 1205, Saer de Quenci was given custody of all his lands, but two years later half the honour was taken from him to reward Simon de Montfort, one of John's continental favourites. Simon held his part of the honour for just a few years before it came into the royal custody; in addition John took the chief castle, Mountsorrel, from Saer's half of Leicestershire. Although Saer was given the earldom of Winchester he would undoubtedly feel aggrieved at such treatment. Further, though Robert FitzWalter was given additional fiefs in 1204, 1207 and 1210, he was deprived of part of his inheritance of the lands of Richard de Lucy, Henry II's justiciar. To add to these insults and deprivations both Robert and Saer had a grudge dating back to 1203, for after their capture by Philip, John refused to pay their ransoms, although he paid those of the other castellans imprisoned at the same time.

21

Northern England during the reign of King John showing some of the important castles

Finally, many barons were under pressure throughout the reign to repay their debts created by the purchase of honours and offices so common in twelfth-century England: John was badly in need of cash to finance the recovery of Normandy, so that any baron who lost the king's favour was immediately subjected to pressure, by improved administrative methods like the Memoranda Rolls, to repay. William de Mowbray had to pay 2,000 marks in 1200 for a judgment in the king's court, and even then the case was not finally settled in his favour. Peter de Brus owed a similar amount for wardships and rights acquired by 1207, while Roger de Montbegon paid 500 marks for his wife, and Nicholas de Stuteville had to pay an exhorbitant relief of 10,000 marks in 1205. Such amercements, incidents, and fines were resented by the barons; they were not originally intended to be used as major sources of royal income, nor were they to be arbitrarily altered at the king's whim. In addition, they gave the king a political hold over his barons since they often had to surrender manors and even hostages to him as guarantees that they would pay. Thus Nicholas de Stuteville had to surrender the valuable manors of Knaresborough and Boroughbridge, John de Lacy the castles of Donnington and Pontefract, until their debts were paid. This made very slow, long-term agreements for repayment, common in the twelfth century, completely impractical, and tightened the king's grip on his tenants in chief.

In addition to the barons many smaller tenants and knights opposed the Crown, especially in the north, though it is clear that many waited until September 1215 before declaring their position. Most knights and subtenants followed the allegiance of their feudal lords, be it for or against the king, but some supported the rebels although their lord was a royalist, especially if the lord had acquired his rights by purchase or custody from the Crown. Ranulf of Chester secured the honour of Richmond in Yorkshire by purchase in 1205 and, although Ranulf was a staunch royalist, the knights of Richmond, led by Ruald FitzAlan, were all in the rebel ranks in 1215 in sympathy with other Yorkshiremen. Rarely did the reverse happen: few knights of rebel barons were royalists.

Many of the rebels, of baronial and knightly rank, were grouped together by contemporaries as 'Aquilonares', 'Norenses' or 'Boreales'. How far and why were the thoughts and actions of these northerners united? The classic study by Professor Holt (**23,** ch. 5) has uncovered a variety of reasons for the grouping. There were of course family ties between the northerners, for Eustace de Vesci and Robert de Ros both married daughters of the king of Scotland, while Richard de Percy, Robert de Ros and Gilbert de Gant were cousins. Yet it is dangerous to assume too much from this, for marriage ties often cemented relationships already formed and several families, like the Percys and Vieuponts, were divided by the rebellion. Northern barons were connected more by the complex landholding system known as feudalism: Roger de Montbegon held land of John de Lacy, Eustace de Vesci held of Gilbert de Gant, Nicholas de Stuteville of William de Mowbray. In addition, all were tenants in chief of the king and as a result they joined together to receive the king on his visits to the north, to conduct the king's justice and administration, and to muster his army. Such occasions as the defence of Normandy in 1203, the expedition to Poitou in 1206 or the Barham Down mobilisation in 1213 were important for meeting and discussion. Sessions of the king's court, when knights served as jurors, coroners, and foresters performed a similar function for the lower social groups. Moreover, the barons' loyalty to each other was confirmed by pledges: if the king imposed a fine on a baron it could be repaid usually only with security or pledges of support from the baron's neighbours, who each took responsibility for part of the debt. Eustace de Vesci, for instance, pledged part of the 500 marks which Roger de Montbegon offered for his wife in 1205. The northern barons who were to be in the rebel ranks in 1215 often acted as pledges for each other, but rarely for colleagues whose political feelings were not similar to their own. They grew up as a united group in a time of political insecurity. They were 'in part the product of the rebellion and the civil war; a political crisis and armed action necessarily canalised policy and opinion. But in part too the rebellion and the civil war were the conscious creation of the Northerners' (**23,** pp. 71–2).

The baronial party comprised two other groups, one in the southeast from East Anglia and Kent, the other in the West Midlands from Herefordshire, Shropshire and Gloucestershire. It is difficult to see any reason why these three areas in particular should have produced such discontent, which appears to stem more from individual grievances against the arbitrary actions of the king. Was King John a tyrant? Did he rule by reference to his own arbitrary will, his *voluntas*, rather than the law, *lex* or *ius*? The chroniclers, of course, have given the king a bad press: the Dunmow annalist records that it was John's wild passion for the daughter of Robert FitzWalter that caused the conspiracy of 1212. Robert supposedly refused to surrender her to him so his castle in London was destroyed and he fled into the arms of Philip Augustus and began to plot against the king. John meanwhile captured the unfortunate girl but because she refused his demands he poisoned her. Wendover describes the crime and punishment of Geoffrey of Norwich in 1212: for speaking against an excommunicated king he was imprisoned in a 'leaden cope' and starved to death.

These are just two examples from many, but it is important to remember that the chronicles are merely reflecting contemporary opinion, in most cases opinion circulating after Runnymede, the civil war and John's death [**doc. 13**]. Rarely do they offer objective surveys based on evidence: they condemn John wholeheartedly, for instance, for selling his kingdom into the slavery of the pope in 1213; they do not consider the obvious political advantage John derived from the move. Richardson and Sayles agree: 'When we have sifted the mass of tales told to John's discredit, the number of crimes and fleshly sins that we can be reasonably certain that he committed are no more than those committed by other kings whose reputation is by no means low and who are judged on their ability to rule. It is by this test that John's reputation should stand or fall' (**50,** p. 336). Unfortunately for John, however, the 'ability to rule' of a medieval king was based largely on his personality, for this was the crucial factor in his relation with his barons. That he could at times be both jealous and suspicious, of friend and foe alike, is borne out clearly by the record evidence; he was also on occasions lustful, though it is difficult to explain the following record on the back of the Oblate Rolls: 'The wife of Hugh de Neville gives the lord king 200 chickens that she may lie one night with her lord Hugh de Neville' (**37,** p. 231). Essentially, however, he was untrustworthy; he did not keep the rules. The taking of hostages was accepted practice in the Angevin system, but John's murder of twenty-eight Welsh hostages at Nottingham in 1212 is difficult to justify. Further the probable murder of Arthur in 1203 aroused baronial suspicion and fear, even among John's friends: Painter can name only five prominent barons who did not fall foul of John at some time during the reign (**37,** p. 229).

One of the critical incidents in John's relations with his barons concerned William de Braose, lord of Bamber, Barnstaple and of a compact Marcher bloc in South Wales and some important territory in Ireland. William was used to power and independence; for although he and John were good friends—William attested many charters between 1200 and 1207—he held his estates in Normandy without interference from royal officials or justices, and in 1208 prevented the king's justiciar in Ireland from emphasising the king's law in Limerick. John became suspicious and jealous of William, the more so since William had paid the Treasury little towards the cost of his privileges, castles or estates. Powicke has added, moreover, that William aroused John's suspicion because he was one of the few who knew the circumstances of Arthur's death (**46,** pp. 469–70). John and William were together at Rouen in 1203 where Arthur was imprisoned, while the only chronicle to record Arthur's death was the Margam annalist who was patronised by William. Powicke believes that William knew too much and was therefore disposed of, and this would certainly account for the death of his wife and son too, though it does not explain why John waited until 1208 to try to silence William.

The evidence for the incident comes from two main sources, the account of Wendover and a letter written by John himself in 1210 and witnessed by many of the important men in the realm [**docs 6, 7**]. Wendover records that in 1208, John, afraid of excommunication and wanting to ensure the loyalty of certain barons, sent soldiers to ask them for hostages. When the soldiers visited William and Matilda, the latter dramatically burst out, 'I will not hand over my sons to our lord King John because he disgracefully killed Arthur his nephew whose custody he had honourably been granted'. William was a little less hostile: 'If I have offended the king in any way I am prepared to give him satisfaction without hostages according to the justice of his court and my equals.' The king was enraged at this and William and Matilda were forced to flee to Ireland, pursued by John in 1210. Powicke may well have tied himself too closely to this chronicle account; other historians prefer the king's official account which emphasises in detail William's refusal to pay his many debts. In 1208, therefore, John sent Gerard D'Athée, the sheriff of Gloucester, to distrain William's Welsh possessions and capture his three castles, the normal procedure in such a case. At this point John and William were still friends, for John returned a priory to William in 1208. But then William tried to recover his three castles by force, was immediately branded as a rebel and forced to flee to

Ireland. Professor Holt prefers this account because it was a financial rather than a political document and 'too many important men put their seals to it for it to be a fabrication' (**23,** p. 186). John had to make an example of William or other barons would refuse his future financial demands; his treatment of William was more in line with Exchequer practice than the arbitrary dealings of an oppressive monarch. But John obviously needed the letter written in 1210 to be well authenticated by signatures: rumours of untrustworthy behaviour could be very damaging and he knew it. Moreover, his treatment of Matilda and her son would certainly arouse baronial hostility and fear: they were offered to William for a ransom of 40,000 marks, and when he refused to pay they were imprisoned in England where they died, according to some reports, of starvation.

To complicate the problem John's barons were intimately connected with the princes of Ireland, Scotland and Wales; both Robert de Ros and Eustace de Vesci acquired lands in Scotland by marrying daughters of William the Lion; the Lacys, Braoses and William Marshal all owned extensive Irish estates, while the Marcher lords of Wales were among the most independent of John's barons. As lord lieutenant John had visited Ireland in 1186 and 1196 and by 1210 much of the land was organised into shires: yet in 1210 it was necessary for John to visit Ireland himself to put pressure on Walter de Lacy and William Marshal to surrender William de Braose, and although the mission failed in this objective it did ensure that future relations were relatively peaceful. The Welsh prince, Llywelyn ab Iorwerth, was far more stubborn: although married to John's daughter Joan, he was the objective of two royal expeditions, persisting in alliance with Philip Augustus [**doc. 9**] and assisting the barons in the capture of Shrewsbury in 1215. Finally, although Scotland was less of a problem, William the Lion always remained an awkward vassal.

THE CONSPIRACY OF 1212

As early as 1209, as we have seen, a group of northern barons had been forming in opposition to John; it was probably in that year too, though it may have been in 1212, that Philip Augustus wrote a letter to John de Lacy, son of Roger de Lacy, who, apart from being constable of the key city of Chester, was also sheriff of the counties of Yorkshire and Cumberland. This letter reveals that young John had friends in the north who planned to make war on the king in both England and Ireland, a possible indication of a connection between John and William de Braose. Moreover, several northern barons had marriage ties with King William of Scotland, among them Eustace de Vesci and Robert de Ros. It may have been his fear of this spreading northern conspiracy that caused John to extract the Marlborough oath of homage from as many freemen as possible in 1209 and to make his expedition to Scotland in the following year. Further, in 1210 John deprived Roger de Lacy of his two northern shires, though there was no evidence or suspicion that he was involved in the conspiracy, and replaced him with two royal favourites, Hugh de Neville and Gilbert FitzRenfrew, men John thought he could trust. In that year, however, there was no need for John to worry: his speedy victory over the Scots and his enforcement of a humiliating peace over King William kept the northern barons quiet, for the time.

There were other, more important, notherners who took offence at John's actions during these years: in 1209 the Exchequer was ordered to collect an aid from the vassals of William de Mowbray to pay William's judicial debts, since he himself had refused to pay; Robert de Vaux had to pay John 750 marks to prevent scandal over his relationship with another man's wife; Richard de Lucy was fined £100 for his poor custody of the royal forest. By 1212, however, it seems that the two organisers of the conspiracy were Eustace de Vesci and Robert FitzWalter: at any rate it was they who fled when the news of the rebellion leaked out to John in August. Professor Holt describes Eustace as 'undoubtedly the most remarkable of the northern lords' but adds that 'there was nothing in his family's history, or his own, before 1212, to make him dependent on the king's good will' (**23,** p. 21). Robert was one of John's trusted castellans at Vaudreuil before betraying the castle to Philip in Philip's crucial attack in 1203. Therefore he has a long record of antagonism towards John: in a quarrel with the abbot of St Albans over nominations to the priory of Binham, Robert, exasperated at the abbot's nerve in putting his own man into the office, plundered the priory and installed his own candidate. The case was brought to the king's court but no decision is recorded: in view of Robert's violent behaviour, it seems unlikely that the verdict would be given in his favour. Two further incidents increased Robert's hatred for

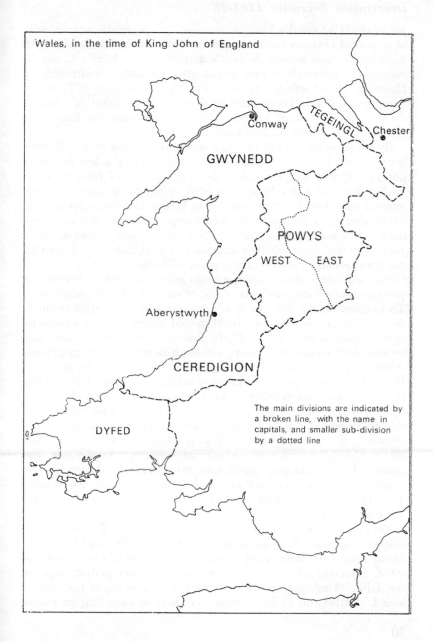

Wales, in the time of King John of England

GWYNEDD

TEGEINGL

Conway

Chester

POWYS

WEST   EAST

Aberystwyth

CEREDIGION

DYFED

The main divisions are indicated by
a broken line, with the name in
capitals, and smaller sub-division
by a dotted line

John: the 'Histoire des Ducs de Normandie', a reliable source, tells of a quarrel between the king and Robert's son-in-law Geoffrey de Mandeville, and reports Robert's arrival at the King's Court to support Geoffrey's claim with 500 knights; secondly, the chronicle of Dunmow priory tells the story of the king's seduction of Robert's daughter Matilda. There may be some truth in either or both of these: Painter inclines towards accepting at least the former as evidence of Robert's quarrel with John (**37**).

By the summer of 1212 the opposition to the king may well have been more widespread than a mere conspiracy of a few northern barons. We can only conjecture from the nature of John's actions during the year. On 1 June writs were issued to the sheriffs for an enquiry into feudal tenures similar to Henry II's *Cartae Baronum* of 1166: after the 'anarchy' of Stephen's reign Henry needed an assessment of the amount of feudal service owed by each tenant in chief. John may well have felt that after so many military expeditions in the previous six years the assessment, still based on Henry's 1166 *Cartae*, was out of date. Again we can only conjecture whether the writs he issued were partly the cause of any conspiracy against him. To begin with, the writs were administered by the sheriffs through the administrative district of the Hundred, rather than by tenants in chief. Consequently, it is unlikely that the barons would feel any immediate pressure from them, although all the sheriffs were themselves tenants in chief and although later similar enquiries made by Henry III, like the one in 1242, were administered first through the Hundred but then regrouped under tenants in chief. Moreover, when feudal service was collected the following year for the expedition to Poitou, it was collected on the old 1166 assessments: consequently the writs of June 1212 were obviously not put into full effect. Finally, feudal military service overseas occupies just one clause (cl. 16) of Magna Carta, and two-thirds of the barons summoned to the expedition to Poitou either went in person or sent their sons. Thus it seems unlikely that the writs had any connection with a conspiracy of 1212.

Yet on the other hand there is no doubt that the events of 1212 helped to increase the general enmity between John and his barons. Many must have heard rumour of the possibility of a new reassessment, especially following the continuous military activity against the Irish, Welsh and Scots for which heavy scutages had beeen levied. Further, on 15 June writs were sent to forty English towns demanding the service due in the event of an invasion from Philip Augustus, and the Pipe Roll for 1212 records an increase in judicial amercements: William Pattishall went on eyre through Staffordshire and Saer de Quenci went through Devon, both exacting heavy fines. There was also a heavy forest eyre, so that the total amercements yielded the Crown nearly £4,500. Finally, there is the story recorded by Coggeshall of the baronial refusal to attend the Poitou expedition in 1213. All this adds up to the general growth of opposition to John during 1212.

It is also important to consider the effect on the barons of the alleged papal deposition of the king in 1212: John's excommunication was certainly published throughout the churches of northern France during that year, but this does not mean that his subjects were released from their obedience or incited to revolt. That development comes from both Wendover and the Burton Annals [**doc. 8**]. The Burton story goes that John met Pandulf and Durand, the papal legates, on 30 August 1211 at Northampton to discuss claims for damages by bishops exiled during the interdict. Both John and Pandulf grew angry when discussions failed and Pandulf in a rage absolved John's subjects of their fealty and threatened that a papal army would invade England, obviously a reference to Philip. Other chroniclers then take up the idea of deposition, but none refers to the Northampton meeting: according to Wendover it was the pope himself who absolved Englishmen of their fealty in 1211 and in the following year Innocent was supposed to have written to Philip to encourage him to take the English throne. In the 'Brut y Tywyso-gion' the pope absolved the three Welsh princes, Llywelyn, Maelgwn and Gwenwynwyn, of their fealty while Coventry records a meeting of the English barons in which a papal letter is read aloud deposing John. Yet even so it seems unlikely that John was deposed by the pope: Professor Cheney has shown that the papal registers reveal no deposition of John, though they include his excommunication and the deposition of Otto. Moreover, Innocent's letter to John '*Auditis Verbis*' [**doc. 12**] of 27 February 1213 agrees on certain terms for peace and warns John that if he does not accept the terms by 1 June he will be deposed. Innocent would hardly write such a letter if John had already been deposed within the previous year. Finally, in letters of November 1212 and March 1213, Innocent refers to John as 'King of England'. Yet, although Innocent did not depose John, the rumour of his having done so, received and used by nearly all the chroniclers, would spread ideas of freedom among the English barons: the Welsh leaders certainly threw off their allegiance and the northern barons may equally well have been influenced by such rumours (**74**).

What then really happened in the summer of 1212? John was preparing for his expedition to Wales and with this in mind he ordered the army to muster in Chester on 19 August. Meanwhile he had gathered together mercenaries from far and near under the captaincy of Normans such as Gerard D'Athée and Engelard de Cigogne (Magna Carta cl. 50) and prepared supplies for the expedition. On 14 August the king was at Nottingham where he executed twenty-eight Welsh hostages, mostly the sons of chieftains, and it was at Nottingham, probably as early as 16 August, but possibly not until the 19th, that he heard of the conspiracy. Wendover dramatises the whole tale: John was sitting in his tent on the night of the 16th when two letters arrived, one from his daughter Joan who was married to Llywelyn, the other from William of Scotland. They were warnings: if John persisted in his Welsh expedition he would be killed, either by the Welsh or by his own barons. The whole army, according to Wendover, was buzzing with rumour.

John acted quickly: on the same day, 16 August, he cancelled the muster at Chester and warned Stephen of Thurnham of the immediate need to protect the royal heir, Prince Henry. He then, according to Wendover, ordered all the barons of whom he was suspicious to send him hostages for their good behaviour. There is no doubt that Eustace de Vesci and Robert FitzWalter promptly fled with their families, the one to Scotland, the other to France. Richard de Umfraville surrendered Prudhoe castle, while David of Huntingdon and Hugh de Balid, also under suspicion, surrendered Barnard Castle and Fotheringay. Moreover, John demanded hostages specifically from Alice Peche, Robert FitzWalter's sister, and fearing the loyalty of the border counties he replaced Robert FitzRoger, not under suspcion but an uncle of John de Lacy, by Philip de Ulecotes as sheriff of Northumberland. On 26 August Philip fortified Alnwick, and by 3 September John was himself at Durham with a band of Brabantine mercenaries. It was undoubtedly his quick action that saved the situation and early in 1213 to prevent any further outbreak he gave Cumberland to Robert de Ros and Yorkshire to Robert de Percy; he also instituted a committee for four northern earls to check the loyalty of the northern sheriffs. Yet

John was still suspicious: other barons suffered, like John FitzHugh who lost the castle at Hertford, and Alexander de Pointon who was deprived of the custody of the Peche barony. Indeed, even after the peace with the papacy in the following year, by which Eustace and Robert were themselves allowed to return, John razed Eustace's castle of Alnwick, a show of strength from an increasingly suspicious monarch.

It is probable that the 1212 conspiracy was no more than the first tentative union of the northern barons: yet the chroniclers have exaggerated it in their usual dramatic fashion. The Bury Chronicle refers to the rape of the Queen, the murder of Prince Richard and the certainty of French invasion. Wendover declares that *all* the barons were in revolt, that John had 'as many enemies as there were magnates'. The Dunstable Annalist quotes a plot to murder the king and replace him with Simon de Montfort. Two further stories stand out: those of Geoffrey of Norwich and Peter of Pontefract. There is obviously some truth in the various monastic legends surrounding Geoffrey of Norwich: Wendover tells how Geoffrey, archdeacon of Norwich, was imprisoned by John in 1209 for refusing to serve an excommunicate king, and died after being encased in a leaden cope. Most of the other chroniclers mention the story, but the man in question was obviously Geoffrey, Justice of the Jews, in Norwich, for the archdeacon of that name lived to become Bishop of Ely in 1225; further the date given by the other chronicles is 1212 after the flight of Eustace and Robert, implying that Geoffrey was imprisoned for a part in their revolt rather than for refusing to serve an excommunicate king. We have no way of knowing the true story. Similarly, with Peter of Pontefract, the chronicles are equally dramatic and equally inaccurate. Coventry has the fullest story, that Peter warned John to correct his behaviour or he would lose his kingdom by Ascension Day 1213. According to Coventry, Peter and his son were executed. The Winchester annalist tells the story and adds that Peter was dragged over Corfe plains and then hanged. None of the other chroniclers add anything on value, butcl early John was now under pressure on many fronts. It was in his own interest to yield to one of his adversaries in order to gain support, ideological rather than military, to tackle the others. He therefore sought a compromise with the pope to a quarrel which went back to 1205.

4 King John and the Church, 1205-13

THE CANTERBURY ELECTION 1205

Medieval secular government was continually troubled by conflict with the Church, on many occasions a conflict of both ideology and personality. In the Holy Roman Empire in the eleventh and twelfth centuries the basic ideological issue, that of *regnum* versus *sacerdotium*, the growing dynastic and political power of the emperor against the universal claims of papal sovereignty, came to a head over the question of lay investiture. By investiture is meant the installation of a cleric into a bishopric and his receipt of a ring and a staff to symbolise his spiritual and pastoral office: the key question was who should install him and confer on him the symbols. Now in the Empire the Saxon emperors had used their bishops as their chief administrators, so that it was important that they should confer the office on men they could trust to do an efficient job. The papacy, on the other hand, particularly Pope Gregory VII, believed that a cleric should be invested by his ecclesiastical superior, the pope. The resulting quarrel, the 'Investiture Contest' was terminated by a compromise at the Concordat of Worms in 1122: the emperor surrendered his powers of investiture of ring and staff but kept two major concessions. All elections were to be conducted in his presence and he would still be allowed to invest the consecrated bishop with the *temporalia* of office. Each see carried with it extensive territory, for which the bishop owed homage to the emperor; the bishop was therefore to be invested in his lands by the emperor. The Concordat, however, solved nothing, for the basic issue of how far the pope could interfere in the political rights of kings, remained unsolved.

In England this was a crucial problem. Henry II put the royal point of view with the Constitutions of Clarendon of 1164 but after Becket's assassination was forced to yield to the Compromise of Avranches. Customarily bishops were elected by the chapter of the cathedral before receiving the *pallium* the spiritual symbol of office, from the pope or his legate, and the *temporalia* from the king. At Clarendon (cl. 11 and 12) Henry had insisted that bishops were barons of the realm and answerable to the king as such. Moreover, elections should take place in the king's presence and the newly elected bishop should pay homage to the king before he could be consecrated by the pope or archbishop [**doc. 2**]. The position was further complicated in elections to the see of Canterbury by the claims of all suffragan bishops to a voice in the election, though in 1193 Hubert Walter had been elected by the cathedral chapter and the king alone. Yet clearly the position was confused, and in two early cases in his reign John had to give way to the pope. The canons of Seez in 1201 elected one of their number to succeed their late bishop, but John refused to accept him; after some quarrelling the chapter split and both parties appealed to Rome. Innocent decided for the candidate of the chapter but John refused to allow him the *temporalia* of the see. He was ultimately forced to give way in May 1203 when Innocent threatened an interdict on Normandy, and John, desperately trying to retain the duchy, was too weak to resist. But the king, significantly, renounced no claims to control elections. Similarly in Armagh in Ireland in the same year John nominated a royal clerk, Humphrey of Tickhill, a man useful as an administrator in Ireland, as his choice. Innocent, however, consecrated a canon of Bangor, Eugenius, and John, so involved elsewhere in 1202–03, was powerless to withstand the pope, though he did not restore the temporalities to Eugenius until 1207.

The see of Canterbury was another matter: the primate of England was traditionally the choice of the king. Men like Lanfranc, Becket and Hubert Walter had been virtually royal appointments, and on the death of Walter in 1205, John had another royal administrator as his candidate, John de Gray, bishop of Norwich; it was the pursuit of John's claim that involved England in the quarrel with the pope, the interdict and a serious problem to complicate the king's other important quest, the recovery of Normandy.

The evidence for the quarrel over the election appears confusing. Wendover tells a long, involved and dramatic tale [**doc. 3**]; he records that Hubert Walter died at Tenham on 13 July 1205, at which John rejoiced since he suspected Hubert of friendship with Philip during the Normandy campaign. Wendover then dramatises the tale of a midnight election, by the younger monks of the Canterbury chapter, of their subprior Reginald, who was then sent secretly to Rome for the pope's blessing. Unfortunately the secret leaked out when Reginald was in Flanders, so that John and the English bishops informed the chapter of their own rights in the case. The chapter divided into two factions, the senior monks accepting the king's choice, John de Gray, and electing him in the king's presence at Canterbury. All three parties, the king, the senior monks and the younger monks, appealed to Rome, and the suffragan bishops too sent an appeal. Innocent on 21 December annulled Reginald's election as informal and John de Gray's since it was conducted after an initial appeal to Rome. The see was therefore vacant. There were, however, Wendover continues, two groups of Canterbury monks present at Rome, and after Innocent had discounted the claims of the king and the bishops to a voice in any election conducted at Rome, they were persuaded to elect Cardinal Stephen Langton to the see of Canterbury and he was consecrated by Innocent at Viterbo on 17 June 1206. Clearly a good story well told.

That there are inaccuracies in Wendover's account is clear from a comparison with some of the other chronicles. The two Canterbury chronicles defend the position of the chapter in the proceedings: the Anonymous Monk of Canterbury records that the chapter deliberated the matter carefully and elected Reginald in the proper manner and sent him to Rome. Gervase of Canterbury [**doc. 4**] comments that it was the king's treachery that caused the impasse: apparently John came to Canterbury on Hubert's death and told the chapter that it could elect one of its own number provided it waited until after 30 November. Meanwhile he sent messengers to Rome to guarantee his own rights in the election, so that when the chapter heard of this treachery they sent Reginald as their representative to Rome to safeguard their rights. There is no mention in Gervase of an election of Reginald, but John heard a rumour to this effect and asked the monks if it was true. They of course denied it and, at John's request, elected John de Gray. Innocent was not satisfied that the election was regular and the monks at Rome were persuaded to elect Langton. This case indicates not only the slow communications and the power of rumour in medieval Europe but also the importance of an election to Canterbury and the confusion caused by some medieval chroniclers.

Only in a recent article by Dom David Knowles has the situation been clarified by the use of Innocent III's letters and papal archives (**94**). Hubert Walter died on 13 July and John immediately went to

Canterbury where he stayed until 20 July. The chapter and the suffragan bishops put to John their claims but John persuaded them to wait until December before electing, so they appealed to Rome. John himself meanwhile wrote to Rome, hoping that Innocent would order the chapter to elect John de Gray. The chapter countered this move by electing Reginald but keeping the election secret until the pope showed his hand. Unfortunately Reginald broke the secrecy on the way to Rome and asked Innocent immediately for confirmation. Innocent eventually postponed a decision and asked the abbots of St Albans and Reading to collect information before 1 May 1206. John heard of Reginald's visit to Rome and asked the monks if they had elected him; they renounced their appeal and elected John de Gray, but Innocent, after a survey of the evidence, summoned fifteen Canterbury monks and attorneys of the king and the bishops to Rome, and in December 1206 Langton was elected. It can be clearly seen how inaccurate and confused are the accounts of Wendover and Gervase, yet how both are partly correct. The story serves as a warning to those who use the medieval chronicler without extreme caution. Knowles's account defends the pope—he only interfered when justice had run its course and a fair solution was otherwise impossible—and slightly vilifies the king, though it must be emphasised that the election of a king's man to Canterbury was the accepted practice.

THE INTERDICT

After Langton's election the pope wrote to John on 20 December 1206 requesting his agreement to Langton; in reply, however, John threatened to cut off the Curia's profits in England and to enforce the Constitutions of Clarendon of 1164 in forbidding English clerics to go to Rome. On 26 May 1207 Innocent wrote again to John pointing out why the king had not been consulted in the election and threatening him with papal disapproval if he should remain obdurate; he also wrote at this time to the bishops of London, Ely and Worcester, encouraging them to urge the king to yield and accept Langton and, if he refused, to lay England under interdict and excommunicate its king. Wendover records that when John heard of this, 'he became nearly mad with rage and broke forth in words of blasphemy against the Pope and his cardinals'. He threatened to confiscate all Church property in England and send all Catholic clerks 'to Rome with their eyes plucked out and their noses slit'. Wendover is unlikely to have accurate evidence for these statements, but John's anger may be presumed. So on 17 November 1207 Innocent explained to the three bishops how the interdict was to be carried out; he also wrote to the magnates and bishops of England urging them to be faithful to Rome. Finally, although negotiations were carried out for a compromise solution during 1208, they were unsuccessful and in the following year the king was excommunicated.

What did the pressure of interdict mean for England and its king? Before 1212 at least it seems that its effects were not particularly harmful. The chroniclers, not surprisingly, have exaggerated the chaos: the prophecy of Peter of Pontefract and the incarceration of Geoffrey of Norwich in his 'leaden cope' discussed in the previous chapter, both reveal the chronicler's desire to incriminate John and increase the tension caused by the interdict. Coggeshall, moreover, tells of John's severe spoliation of religious houses in 1210 and of his refusal to allow Cistercian abbots to attend their annual chapter at Citeaux, and states that in 1212 'John demanded charters from all the clergy of England in which they were made to testify falsely that, whatever John stole from them violently, they gave graciously and of their own free will'. Wendover develops the situation still further; he records how in 1209 the mayor and people of Oxford hung three clerks whose colleague had killed a woman and fled, the punishment taking place 'at the command of the king in contempt of clerical privilege'. Wendover also tells the story of Alexander the mason who, after publishing sermons in support of the king, was deprived of his benefice by the pope and driven into poverty to be mocked wherever he went. As Professor Cheney has pointed out (**75**), some of these tales are not in themselves unlikely; but the general picture of tension and chaos in England which they reveal is highly exaggerated, since several could have occurred at any time, not just during an interdict. Further the chronicles record just one side of the coin, for John was as generous to the Church during the interdict as he was for the rest of his reign (**50,** p. 347).

The terms of the interdict were hard: Cheney has shown how the pope's original instruction, that no divine service was to be performed except baptism and penance of the dying, created difficulties of interpretation (**75**). For instance, how can a priest baptise when he is not allowed to consecrate the chrism? Local practice therefore varied: according to one source baptism was carried out at the child's home, while another source depicts it behind closed doors in church [**doc. 10**]. In 1209 Innocent allowed conventual churches to celebrate mass behind closed doors, Wendover says at Langton's request. But how many churches were 'conventual'? Further, Cheney believes that, as far as the evidence goes, the bishops and clergy remaining in England kept the terms of the interdict: there was no Christian burial, no mass, and no last sacrament for the dying, at least before 1212 when it seems that Innocent relented on this last restriction. The mass of Christian faithful in England would therefore suffer a great deprivation and the chroniclers may well be reflecting contemporary opinion in laying the blame on the king. John himself remained unmoved: he continued his charities to the Church, such as the 1212 gifts to monasteries and the building of three new abbeys in 1213. Everyday Church administration, pleas of advowsons about the presentation to Church livings and final concords, remained unbroken, and felonious clerks continued to be removed to Church courts for trial. The elections to four bishoprics occurred during the interdict and, although many bishops did seek voluntary exile abroad, the English Church was used to long vacancies and absentee bishops and had developed the machinery to cope without them. It is true that there were no appeals to Rome during the interdicts, no church synods and no visitations of bishops, but, these apart, the administration of the Church continued unimpaired. Further, although John did impose some 'economic sanctions' on the lands of exiled bishops and vacant sees, his profits were limited. A full discussion of how far the interdict affected the king appears in chapter 7 below.

The chief political effect of the excommunication of the king was that no Catholic subject ought to have contact with him in any way. Obviously this created a dilemma for John's barons and bishops in particular; to which institution did they owe their obedience, *regnum* or *sacerdotium*? The pope's letter of 21 November had urged them to be faithful to Rome; obviously this was why many bishops fled the realm. There is no evidence, though, that any of the barons observed the pope's wishes, though John's insistence on the oath of homage from all free tenants, taken at Marlborough, and from the Welsh princes at Woodstock, in 1209, indicates that he was determined to emphasise to Innocent that he still had political control of his own realm. Further, a letter in the Chancery rolls reveals that

John insisted on the homage of the Irish barons who declared: 'We are prepared to defend his privileges and go with him in life and death.' Moreover, in 1212 John was forcing his barons to put their seals to his letters patent sent out to 'all Christ's faithful'. Indeed it was only in this year, with rumours of the pope's deposition of the king, the baronial conspiracy in the north, and the preparations of Philip Augustus to invade England, that John began to doubt his political security.

The only really serious attempt to achieve a peaceful solution to the inderdict was made during the visit of Pandulf, a cardinal, and Durand, a Templar, to England on the pope's behalf in June 1211. At the end of August they met John in confident mood after his successful Welsh expedition with the brief from Innocent that they should 'warn the king to make satisfaction to God and the Church according to the form prescribed below after much deliberation between us and his royal envoys' [**doc. 11**]. They were to demand John's public surrender, either in the form of letters patent or a public oath. John was further to yield full restitution to Langton and the exiled bishops and if this were not done within one month the nuncios were to return to Rome. In addition Innocent wrote to John informing him that he would 'make heavy our hand aginst you' if John refused to yield; presumably this refers to the threat of deposition and the encouragement of a 'crusade' by Philip Augustus against England. John's reply to these 'compromise' terms is unknown, though the Burton Annals give a long, probably fictitious, account of a conversation in which Pandulf deposes John. What is known is that the nuncios returned to the continent in September unrewarded, so that when Innocent next proposed terms for John's submission, in February 1213, they were much harsher [**doc. 12**].

JOHN'S SUBMISSION TO ROME

By the end of 1212, the king was ready to sumit to the pope. Wendover attempts to assess the reasons for his submission: 'Then on the Pope's authority, the Archbishop together with the Bishops of London and Ely . . . commanded all people and especially the King of France, for the remission of their sins, that they should all attack England together and put King John from off his throne and, with

Papal approval, choose another more worthy in his place.' Wendover adds that John feared for his own salvation and also feared the desertion of his barons if Philip did invade. Much of this again is pure fabrication: there is no evidence to corroborate his account of direct papal encouragement for Philip's invasion, and if John feared for his own salvation, why did he wait until 1213 before submitting. Yet there may be some substance to Wendover's views: John would know that even the rumour of papal deposition could cause his ruin, while the internal situation in England and the home counties must have worried him. Moreover, the 'Histoire des Ducs de Normandie', a very reliable contemporary source, states that the prophecy of Peter of Wakefield frightened John because he knew the hatred that many Englishmen bore him.

Finally the key to the situation may well have lain in Europe: in 1210 Otto, John's nephew, had been excommunicated and papal support given to the Hohenstaufen candidate for the Empire, Frederick II. Now the Hohenstaufen were in alliance with Philip of France, so that there was a strong trio hostile to John. Painter believes that John was not afraid of Philip's invasion since many French knights were in the Albigensian Crusade and Philip himself had to contend with the revolt of his nephew the count of Toulouse and the disaffection of the Counts of Boulogne and Flanders, both of whom received money fiefs from John (**95**). John, however, must surely have feared the man who captured Normandy from him and gave refuge to English rebels like Robert FitzWalter; however, with the removal of the ideological support of the pope Philip would have no reason to invade England.

In November 1212, therefore, John sent an embassy of six men to Rome. Three were captured by Philip on the way, but three did get through, the Cistercian abbot of Beaulieu, Alan Martel the Templar, and one whose name is not known; all three were members of international church organisations whom Philip would not dare to molest. They told the pope that John would accept the terms offered by Pandulf and Durand in 1211, and Innocent wrote them in more detail in a letter to John on 27 February 1213 [**doc. 12**]. The terms proposed were harsher than those of 1211. John was given a time limit: he must accept the terms by 1 June. Further, Innocent gave full details of financial compensation, not just for Canterbury but for the whole English Church, and in addition John had to accept the return of Eustace de Vesci, and Robert FitzWalter. Any problems of

41

interpretation of the terms were to be settled by the king in discussion with Pandulf, who was to relax the interdict only when all the terms had been fulfilled. Other letters from the pope to Langton and the bishops in March 1213 added even greater severity: any cleric who had served the king during the interdict must go to Rome for absolution, no individual cleric could make agreements with the king over Church lands, and finally if John should ever break the terms of agreement imposed on 27 February, then Langton should immediately replace the sentences of interdict and excommunication and refuse to anoint John's heirs.

The Chancery rolls for May and June reveal that John was prepared to accept these terms. At Dover on 13 May John surrendered his crown to Pandulf, thus fulfilling the prophecy of Peter of Wakefield. John did more than this though, for he paid homage to the pope and surrendered England to papal overlordship. He became in fact a feudal vassal of the pope, a shrewd move, since he thus gained active papal support against Philip Augustus, and, for 1,000 marks per annum, the support of the pope against any rebellious barons. Moreover, Langton was permitted to return on 24 May with the statement 'You shall be treated as you ought', and John promised to abide by the pope's terms on the signatures of the archbishop of Dublin, the bishops of Norwich—a great irony—and Worcester and twelve important barons. Langton then absolved John of excommunication on 20 July at Winchester; Simon Langton, Robert FitzWalter and Eustace de Vesci were invited to return and their lands were restored, while Giles de Braose, bishop of Hereford, was given back all the lands which John had confiscated during the interdict. Finally the sentence of outlawry passed on exiled clergy was revoked and several bishops were reseised of their lands, although John made as yet no full restitution as demanded by the 27 February letter from the pope.

Few contemporaries disapproved of John's act, though thirteenth-century opinion later condemned him for surrendering England to the pope. Walter of Coventry states that 'to many people it seemed ignominious and a yoke of servitude', while a certain monk of Rievaulx, obviously a strong patriot, is supposed to have exclaimed, 'Christ Jesus, destroy this shame, quickly break this yoke'. Wendover and Matthew Paris also express their disappointment at such a humiliation. But really there was nothing unusual in subjecting a kingdom to the feudal overlordship of Rome: twelve lay barons had signed John's charter, thus giving it their approval, while other kingdoms like Hungary, Sicily and Leon were also papal vassals. Painter indeed has suggested that the English barons knew that the move was a political one made by a cunning king (**37,** p. 194).

John was certainly not worried by any criticism in the middle of 1213 for he had two other problems on his mind. He had already secured the support of the counts of Flanders and Boulogne in his attempts to defend England against Philip and also to plan the recovery of Normandy; further in May he was fortifying Winchelsea and assembling his army at Barham Down and at the end of the month he sent a large force to Bruges, in response to Ferrand's appeal, to defeat Philip's fleet at Damme. It was this, together with Pandulf's letter to Philip warning him against attacking a papal vassal, which finally forestalled any plans Philip may have had to attack England.

John's second problem was that of reparations to the Church. To discuss the details Cardinal Nicholas of Tusculum was sent to England, though John was determined to drive a hard bargain since his plans for the recovery of Normandy involved high expenditure. As a safeguard he had persuaded all the monasteries to sign a letter, prepared by his chancery, to the effect that any money the king had received from them during the interdict was given 'in good spirit and entirely of our own free will'. Unfortunately for John, Langton heard of the device and told Innocent, who insisted that it be null and void; John overcame this later by the preparation of a second letter by which the monasteries agreed that they had received the full amount in restitution from the king. Moreover, John's agents may well have slowed down the machinery for estimating the amount of reparation due: three royal agents, plus a number of clerical officials in each diocese, were to investigate all custodians of Church property. When Cardinal Nicholas arrived in October he realised that this would be a very lengthy process, so at a conference held in London he and King John agreed at a total figure of 100,000 marks and although the bishops disapproved the pope accepted the compromise and ordered Nicholas to relax the interdict as soon as the money was paid. John was not satisfied and appealed to the pope, whereupon he was ordered to pay 40,000 marks to include all previous payments before the relaxation of the interdict and 12,000 marks per annum thereafter. However, since Nicholas allowed John 13,000 marks remission on the original 40,000 marks and since the civil war occurred within the next year it is unlikely that John actually repaid very much. Perhaps this is a measure of John's skill more than his conduct of military campaigns. The interdict was finally relaxed in the middle of 1214.

5 The Growth of Hostility to John, 1213–15

THE EFFECTS OF JOHN'S EXPEDITION, 1213–14

In the summer of 1213 John was preparing his forces for an expedition to Poitou; he had surrendered to the Church and received Innocent's assistance in preventing Philip's invasion. Now he himself had to plan the recovery of Normandy, the basic theme of his reign. He was prevented from undertaking an expedition in 1213 because many northerners refused to send their quotes for the campaign; here we see the beginning of concerted opposition to the king. Barons' reasons varied: according to Wendover many 'were unwilling to follow the Lord King unless he were first absolved of his excommunication'. This may have been an astute move since Eustace de Vesci, Robert FitzWalter and Giles de Braose, three key figures, were allowed to return by the papal terms imposed on John. Coventry, on the other hand, does not mention the excommunication: 'Many of the princes dared to oppose the king more as men who would be annoyed by a long journey and couldn't easily agree to the length of the expedition since their resources were already exhausted and their expenses would be great.' Coggeshall agrees with Coventry: the barons owed no service outside the realm and their resources were exhausted. The latter would certainly be true, for every year since 1209 had seen some expedition or scutage and during May 1213 John's army had been assembled at Barham Down for the permitted forty days of feudal service before John developed the idea of going to Poitou.

It is, however, on the legal problem that most historical attention has focused. Did the king have the legal right to ask for military service overseas and for longer than forty days? Professor Holt believes that those who refused to serve 'were denying their primary responsibility as military tenants of the king. . . . Their actions were deliberately provocative' (23, p. 89). The chief northerners knew this, for William de Mowbray, Robert de Ros, Richard de Percy, Peter de Brus and Roger de Montbegon, all later members of the Twenty-Five, had all served without murmur on previous occasions and had paid their scutage in 1205. Some may well have had a legal case in 1213 if they were tenants by cornage, which confined military service responsibility to the Scottish border and allowed a cash payment instead of service overseas; however, since most had served in or paid scutage for the previous expedition to Poitou this ought not to be emphasised. Holt suggests that, reinforced by the return of Eustace de Vesci and believing the submission to Rome to be a humiliation, the barons would have discussed the situation while waiting at Barham Down and decided to use John's evident weakness to force a concession from him (**23**). As a result of their pressure John was forced to promise general reform in the hope that, pacified, the northerners would accompany his Poitou expedition in the following year. Success in that campaign would give John the strength to defeat his barons at home, but this was a considerable gamble for a king who had had little success hitherto in major military ventures.

The reforms promised by the king were discussed on four occasions when the barons grouped together for various purposes in the latter part of 1213. Wendover and Coggeshall both mention that when Langton absolved John on 20 July, John renewed his coronation oath, in which he promised to restore the good laws of Henry I and banish all evil customs. These laws of Henry I [**doc. 1**] became, according to the chroniclers, one of the main points by which the baronial party took their stand, as though the whole governmental system had been corrupted by the Angevins from 1154 onwards. They cropped up, indeed, at the second meeting at St Albans, in which, during John's absence in Guernsey, Geoffrey FitzPeter and the bishop of Winchester held discussions with Langton and the bishops. Thirdly, although even the notorious Wendover admits that the story is no more than a rumour, Langton is said to have taken the barons aside at a sermon in St Paul's in August and told them, 'You have heard how, when I absolved John at Winchester, I compelled him to swear that he would abolish unjust laws and revive the good laws of Edward the Confessor and cause them to be shared by all in the kingdom. Now I have found a charter of Henry I through which you may recover all your liberties and return to your former state' [**doc. 19**]. Finally the barons met the king himself at Wallingford in November, when John promised again to restore their ancient liberties; such promises were shortlived for on 15

November John summoned the barons to Oxford unarmed, while insisting that the knights of the realm also attend, fully armed. The authenticity of these meetings must be doubtful since we have only the testimony of the chroniclers, and Wendover alone among them emphasises the charter of Henry I before 1215.

Yet it may well have been about this time that the Unknown Charter of Liberties first appeared. This consisted of the charter of Henry I plus a list of concessions based on the charter to the effect that the king promises not to sell justice or imprison anyone unjustly. It seems in fact a commentary on the king's oath taken at Winchester in July 1213. The charter also contains a clause limiting foreign service in Poitou, and for this reason some authorities date it somewhere between the end of 1213 and the middle of 1214 (**38, 47**). To be more precise it could be a product of the discussions at Wallingford when the Poitou scutage was, according to the Dunstable annalist, one of the key issues. It is important to remember, however, that it may never have been issued, for it was no more than a rough draft, a series of notes for discussion. Beyond that, it is impossible to date it more accurately. Professor Holt (**24,** pp. 151 and 297–300) and other authorities place it somewhere in the political discussions of 1215, emphasising that the differences between it and the Articles may indicate the variety of baronial opinion.

Significantly, at the end of 1213 John became aware of the growth of opposition among the barons and began to look for support, not only among the knights at Oxford, but among the barons too. He made concessions to various East Anglians in the hope of dividing them from the northerners: the hostage daughter of Earl Richard of Clare was released and Geoffrey de Mandeville was given the whole of his barony and allowed to marry the king's former wife Isabella of Gloucester; Robert FitzWalter's losses during his exile were assessed, presumably with a view to repayment; John de Lacy's inheritance was returned to him and grants of land were made to Thomas of Moulton. Moreover, the king made changes in shire administration by installing loyal familiars, John Marshal and Peter FitzHerbert in Lincolnshire and Yorkshire. He thus hoped to check the hostility, of the north and secure his position for his coming campaign to Poitou.

From 9 February to 15 October 1214 John was absent from England, thus allowing those barons who remained at home freedom to conspire and eventually, through his failure at La Roche aux Moins and Bouvines, increasing their distrust of his kingship. It is instructive to see which barons went to Poitou and which remained at home, and since the official records are very full on this point, they can be used to corroborate the views of Coggeshall and Coventry, who emphasise that opposition to the expedition came from the north. In 1214 southern and East Anglian barons were by and large loyal: Saer de Quenci sent his son to Poitou while Roger Bigod sent the required quota of knights. Both, moreover, were given permission to collect their scutage from their subtenants, as were Richard de Muntfichet, William de Llanvallei and William of Huntingfield, Robert FitzWalter, William de Albini and Earl Richard of Clare. Some of the northerners approved of the expedition too: Robert de Ros and Simon de Kyme sent their sons, while Nicholas de Stuteville, John de Lacy and Maurice de Gant are accounted in the Prest Rolls for payments to their knights. All these men, important baronial leaders in 1215, were clearly prepared to support the king at the beginning of 1214. In fact only six northerners refused: Eustace de Vesci, Peter de Brus, Richard de Percy, Roger de Montbegon, Robert Grelley, and William Mowbray. Thus Painter has argued that the scutage and expedition did little in themselves to create the opposition to John since two-thirds of the English earls served or sent their representatives and those barons who refused to go were mostly implacable enemies of the king before 1214 (**37**).

If, however, we compare the opposition to John in February 1214 with that of October 1214, there can be little doubt that his absence and failure did at least foster discontent, even if they were not primarily responsible for it. Evidence for this comes from many sources. In the middle of the campaign John wrote home from La Rochelle to encourage any barons who had not originally come to Poitou to help him now; he promised too that all would be forgiven if they did! Clearly none of the six did send help for Peter des Roches, the justiciar, distrained their stock in John's absence, but postponed the case until his return in November. Moreover, there is in the Public Record Office a letter from Innocent III to Eustace de Vesci dated 5 November 1214 requesting Eustace to support John in Poitou and not to conspire against him in his absence. It is likely that other dissidents received a similar letter and that the letters were sent at John's request now that his campaign in Poitou had so obviously failed. Further, the king's policy of concessions to the English Church implies his need for support on his return from Poitou: on 21 November he made the famous grant of free election [**doc. 20**] thus finally yielding, in theory at least, much of the ground over which the interdict was fought. Again, he confirmed the bishop of Lincoln in his lands and gave the patronage of Rochester to the see of Canterbury and that of Thorney abbey to the bishop of Lincoln.

The most significant indication of baronial opposition following the failure in Poitou comes from the collection of scutage in September. All tenants in chief who had been given permission to collect the scutage from their subtenants were to present the money to Peter des Roches on 9 September. There were no payments at all from Yorkshire and Lancashire, while many East Anglians like Robert FitzWalter, Earl Richard of Clare, Earl Roger Bigod, Earl William of Arundel, and Hubert de Burgh also refused to pay. Essex, Hertfordshire, Norfolk and Suffolk are all totally blank on the Pipe Roll, while individual blank entries appear for every county, though this must not be emphasised since there is even a blank against the justiciar himself (**23**). Clearly, however, there is much concerted action and conspiracy here, and it is at this time that, according to Wendover at least, the barons met at Bury St Edmunds, 'for when they had earlier begun secretly to conspire, they had received a certain charter of Henry I from Stephen, the archbishop of Canterbury, as we have already shown'. Wendover states that if John refused to grant the laws and liberties of Edward the Confessor and Henry I contained in this charter, then the barons swore over the great altar that they would make war on him and break off their fealty until they were given these liberties 'in a charter under his seal' [**doc. 14**]. Wendover, shows here the benefits of both dramatic ability and hindsight but there is little evidence to corroborate his picture. Coggeshall points to the growth of a baronial party and the interest in the charter of Henry I at the end of 1214, while Coventry reports a meeting between king and barons at which the presence of Langton and the charter of Henry I helped to cool the bitter feelings between the parties. What is, therefore, very clear is that by the end of 1214 there was an amorphous body of opposition to the king: John agreed to meet the hostile element in London at Epiphany 1215.

But first he had to prepare his own party. As soon as the opposition to the Poitou scutage was known in 1214 Peter des Roches ordered Philip of Ulecotes to restock and fortify all royal castles in his charge; possibly other castellans received similar orders. When John returned from Poitou and saw the situation he summoned his Poitevin mercenaries under Fawkes de Breauté, and ordered several key castles like Nottingham and Knaresborough to be fortified and partly rebuilt. According to the Pipe Roll 16 John, he was also counting on the shire administration to help him; for between 1212 and 1214 ten shires changed hands and four changed hands twice. Although some of these, like the removal of Robert de Vieupont from Wiltshire were purely matters of routine, since Robert kept Devon and soon took charge of John's son Richard, others, like the removal of Hubert de Burgh and Gilbert FitzReinfrey, were to secure political support from men John could trust in important offices. Robert de Ros, for instance, a favourite now though later a rebel, replaced Robert de Percy in the crucial county of Yorkshire (**23**). Finally John increased his reliance on Innocent III and the English Church, for not only did he make concessions to the English bishops outlined above, but he also asked Innocent to send letters to the conspirators urging them to be loyal. John also sent Walter Mauclerc, a royal clerk, to Rome to act as his representative there and to forestall any agents which the barons might send [**doc. 21**]. During the fateful months that led up to Magna Carta the support of Innocent was crucial to both John and the 'army of God', especially perhaps because of the powerful influence of Langton.

THE EVE OF MAGNA CARTA

King John met the baronial opposition in London, as agreed, at Epiphany, 6 January 1215, when nearly all those barons now in arms were present except for Eustace de Vesci. Most of the chroniclers agree about the meeting and for once there seems little reason to doubt Wendover's statement that the barons sought the laws and liberties of Henry I; nothing came of the meeting but the chroniclers record that a truce was made until a second discussion could be held on the Sunday after Easter, 26 April. In the meantime both parties prepared their legal and military defence. On 8 January John sent more representatives to Rome to appeal for legal support from Innocent and on 13 January he sent to the pope a copy of the Charter to the Church which he had granted the previous November, and the barons, not to be outdone, also sent their agents to Rome. On 19 February John granted safe-conducts to some of the barons to meet Langton and William Marshal at Oxford on 22 February, but the notice may have been too short for none of the barons attended the meeting; perhaps they distrusted the mediating influence of both Langton and the Marshal. Then John produced another ingenious masterstroke when on 4 March he took the Cross, led according to Wendover 'by fear rather than by devotion'. John, however, could afford just to sit and wait: legally he was emphasising his rightful position as being guaranteed by his submission to the pope and now by his promise to go on crusade. Legally the barons were his subjects and their rebellion would put them in the wrong. The twelfth century was a great age for the study of law, and in the eyes of the law John would undoubtedly win; so confident was he indeed that on 13 March he ordered some of his Poitevin mercenaries to return home, 'because the business for which they were required has been concluded'; perhaps he also hoped to conciliate some of the barons by the move. Certainly he was still trying to compromise with them, for he offered to redress any 'burdensome' grievances caused by his own or his brother's reign; but the barons refused. Professor Holt has suggested that perhaps some of the barons accepted the offer and so John had the confidence to dismiss his mercenaries (**24,** p. 143).

Meanwhile both royal and baronial representatives had arrived at Rome and the legal debate began in earnest. Since it took from four to six weeks to make the journey to Rome the pope's verdict was of legal importance, but not of much practical use, since in two or three months the situation in England may have changed completely. On 19 March the pope gave his opinion by despatching three letters to England, known as the 'Triplex Forma Pacis', one to the clergy and bishops reproaching them for not mediating in the quarrel, one to the barons condemning all conspiracy against the king and urging respectful petition as an alternative, and a third to the king himself praising his surrender of the kingdom, promising 'Apostolic help and favour in whatever we shall see pertaining to your royal honour and profit', and encouraging the king to treat his barons justly. This papal solution, emphasising the legality of John's position, applied to the situation in England in early January: it reached the king and the barons some time in the early part of May. In the meantime John had failed to keep his promise to meet the barons for further discussions at Northampton on Low Sunday, 26 April, though he did allow safe conducts to baronial leaders to meet Langton and William Marshal at Brackley and after discussion they sent their grievances to the king at Wallingford.

The evidence for this whole period is very contradictory and prejudiced: as Professor Holt has said, 'events occurred so rapidly that contemporaries quickly became confused' (**24,** p. 145). The historian relies largely on royal and papal letters for his chronology, like the king's account presented in a letter to the pope on 29 May [**doc. 16**] and papal accounts which appear in letters dated 18 June and 24 August. Moreover, the chroniclers only add to the confusion so that what happened next is largely conjecture: Professor Cheney (**77**) and Richardson and Sayles (**50,** appendix V) believe that the 'Triplex Forma Pacis' arrived in England at the beginning of May and it is likely that the barons published their *diffidatio* or feudal renunciation of the king at Reading on 5 May. Certainly they were in arms at this time, for a group of barons began a siege of Northampton on that date. The question remains, why did the discussions break down and war begin? It is possible that on receipt of the pope's verdict the baronial leaders knew they had no chance in law and so decided on rebellion; it is also possible that the king had refused the Brackley schedule of grievances, and this indeed would be likely if it was as extreme as the earlier Unknown Charter of Liberties. On 6 May John offered his own compromise suggestion, that he would reform any evil customs of his own and his brother's reign; three days later he proposed a joint committee of four barons, four royal representatives and the pope to arbitrate in the quarrel, but the barons knew that after the papal verdict of 19 March they would get little favour from the pope, especially after John's promise to take the Cross. Moreover, at the same time as he was offering them a compromise he asked Langton, probably on 8 May, to excommunicate them and when Langton refused he wrote to the pope to request that Langton be made to do it. The barons were therefore suspicious of arbitration and war was imminent.

John, in fact, had for some time been making active military preparations, in addition to securing support from the pope and certain sections of the baronage (**23,** pp. 104–6). He had despatched the mercenaries who had arrived from Poitou around the English castles, at least ten of which were being refortified. Peter de Maulay was ordered to surround the town of Doncaster with a palisade, while Philip Mark at the key town of Nottingham had been receiving reinforcements and supplies since the previous October, and Hugh de Neville's garrison at Scarborough was also increased. Even more foreign mercenaries arrived from Poitou, the men of Savary de

Mauléon, so that if John's plans for legal support failed he would be well able to defend his position by force. He also tried to strengthen his political position in the north by installing William de Fors in Skipton with the aim of developing royalist influence in Yorkshire, by granting the honour of Tickhill to Ralf of Lusignan, and by installing Peter de Maulay in the Doncaster area with a good marriage and complete remission on all his debts to the king until further notice. John was also still trying to catch the uncommitted, particularly Robert de Ros and John de Lacy, both of whom were important northern castellans. Robert was given the farm of Carlisle to pay for the upkeep of the castle guard, while John de Lacy, the constable of Chester, was pardoned of his debts in March, again until further notice. This was a technique by which the king hoped to retain the loyalty of such key men for it was now clear that the barons had rejected his proposals of 6–10 May.

On 12 May John sent writs to the sheriffs ordering the seizure of lands and chattels belonging to his enemies and two days later he began granting rebel land to his own supporters, which, though difficult to carry out in practice, would certainly harden the opposition. Wendover reports that the siege of Northampton failed for lack of siege engines, but that the barons succeeded in taking Bedford. From there they moved south to Ware and then to London, in response to messengers who told them that the city would surrender. According to Wendover they marched through the city gates on 17 May while the mass of the populace was at divine service, and then issued letters to all the royalist barons like William Marshal, William of Warenne and William of Salisbury to urge them to join the rebel cause. According to Wendover 'most' of them did so. Walter of Coventry in reporting the build-up of the baronial party refers to the support they received from Llywelyn and Alexander, though he admits it is only a rumour; the rising in Devonshire and the capture of Exeter; and the eventual capture of Northampton and Lincoln at the beginning of June. Coventry was accurate about the Welsh princes; since most of the Marcher lords were royalists like Walter de Lacy and William Marshal, the princes would join the rebels (**31**). Llywelyn rose and captured Shrewsbury in the middle of May in company with Giles de Braose, bishop of Hereford. The crucial event, however, was the capture of London, since it gave the barons some influence over the royal administration as well as much prestige. Coggeshall records that the news of its capture

53

persuaded 'many daily to go over to the army of God', including the knights of many barons who remained loyal. It was certainly at this very late stage that certain members of the Twenty-Five like John de Lacy and Robert de Ros finally threw in their lot with the opposition. The capture of London gave the baronial party the semblance of success, so that men who remained uncommitted until they saw which way the wind was blowing now joined the rebels. This was crucial; John was 'besieged with such great terror that he never left Windsor'.

The king was now confronted with a powerful opposition. Painter has tried to establish the size of the parties at this time (**37,** pp. 296–9). The rebels according to his figures held thirty-nine of the 197 baronies in England, but of the twenty-eight most powerful barons in 1199, thirteen were rebels in 1215 and while only thirty-nine baronies were held by the rebels, only about the same number were held by known royalists. The evidence is very limited but Painter can conclude 'that the baronage was essentially divided between the two parties' though 'the great mass . . . stayed out of the affair altogether' since the majority did not cling to either side, preferring instead to maintain the security of their own estates. However, the opposition was strong enough for the king to issue on 25 May a safe conduct to Saer de Quenci, earl of Winchester, to come to his court to discuss terms on the barons' behalf; two days later he issued similar safe conducts to Langton and the barons' representative to attend discussions at Staines, and on 8 June this was extended to 10 June and on that date to 15 June. The two sides were clearly trying to reach a suitable compromise and it is likely that the Articles of the Barons were introduced at this time as a suitable basis for discussion. On 29 May the king again suggested to Saer de Quenci that they put their quarrel to the pope for arbitration, but there was little chance that the barons would agree, for, after their *diffidatio*, their legal position was very flimsy compared with that of the king (**24,** p. 147).

The historian must be very critical of the traditional view of the 'making of Magna Carta' by which the barons were thought to have come to Runnymede on 15 June to present the 'Articles of the Barons' on the basis of which discussion took place so that Magna Carta could be signed on 19 June. Professor Holt (**84**) and Professor Cheney (**77**) have both criticised this view and have recently received support from Professor Galbraith (**81**); they believe that the Articles of the Barons were drawn up as a result of discussion before 15 June and presented as a compromise, a more moderate basis for discussion than the Unknown Charter. Discussions on the Articles lasted until 19 June when a firm peace was made by the kiss of peace and the renewal of homage. This would be far more decisive than the sealing of the Great Charter which was probably not done until 23 June. The Patent Rolls between 19 and 24 June reveal that the 'firm peace' was put into effect: letters ordered the release of hostages and prisoners, and the surrender of castles like the one at York which was released to 'our sweet and faithful William de Mowbray'. Letters commanded the return of foreign mercenaries from Dover to the Continent and the return of rights of guardianship such as Richard de Muntfichet's custody of the forest of Essex. John's soldiers were paid off, he quit himself of his debts and he returned all the confiscated land of his opponents, but as we shall see later that was not the end of the matter.

One important question on the events of June 1215 remains unanswered: why did John yield to the baronial demands? Considering how extreme many of the clauses of the charter were, it must have seemed foolish to surrender. Did John genuinely feel himself in too tight a corner? Certainly many of the barons joined the rebels late in May and June: John de Lacy was known to be loyal on 2 May while William de Fors is first revealed as a rebel when his name is listed among the Twenty-Five. Certainly the baronial opposition was widespread throughout England and supported by Welsh and Scots too, so that John, as the chroniclers were later to do, may have exaggerated the critical nature of his own position and the almost inevitable victory of the barons (**24,** p. 139). Certainly he would be dismayed by the loss of important towns like Northampton, Lincoln and Exeter and of course London, as well as the defection of key castles like Chester and Carlisle. But does all this explain his surrender? He had written to Innocent III on 29 May explaining the whole series of events and vilifying the barons [**doc. 16**]. Perhaps by surrendering temporarily—for surely he had no intention of keeping to the terms of the charter?—he could gain more time, as he had done in January, until an official condemnation of the baronial conspiracy could arrive from Rome and an interdict be placed on the barons' lands and their persons excommunicated. As Holt (**24,** p. 147) has emphasised, the king believed he had the law on his side, so that, by exacting a charter from their king under duress, the barons would put themselves even more in the wrong. Finally John's great problem in June 1215 was that he no longer knew who was loyal and who was conspiring; after the recent defection of John de Lacy and William de Fors, he would be confused. A letter in the Close Rolls for 29 May reveals: 'If Hugh de Beauchamp is an enemy and with our enemies, then his lands in Cornwall are granted to Hasculf de Sulleny.' The fact was that John needed a respite just to find out what the position was.

Part Three

ANALYSIS 1204–15

6 The King's Government

Throughout the months which had led up to Magna Carta the baronial party had laid great emphasis on the laws of Edward the Confessor and the charter of Henry I, which Wendover records (though this is unlikely) were given to them by Langton at St Paul's [**doc. 14**]. This use of Saxon and early Norman law was crucial to the barons for it was a return to the 'good old custom' which the Angevins, in their tyranny, had supposedly corrupted. As we have already shown, during the early months of 1215 both king and barons sought a legal decision from the pope: the king legally was in a far better position than his adversaries, especially after his submission to the pope, his taking the Cross in March 1215 and the baronial defiance in May. The only legal ground on which the barons could stand was the charter of Henry I [**doc. 1**]: their Unknown Charter of Liberties was based on it; so, according to the chroniclers, were their meetings with John before June 1215. By his charter Henry I promised 'I shall remove all evil customs by which this realm of England is unjustly oppressed.' Professor Holt has emphasised the significance of the word *injuste* (**84**): the basic baronial demand was for just treatment by legal procedure and the only standard of legal procedure that they possessed had been laid down, before the Angevin despotism, by Henry I. Thus when clause 40 of Magna Carta stated 'To no one will we sell, to no one will we deny or delay right or justice', it symbolised the essence of the baron's demands. To men of the twelfth century there was no distinction between *lex* and *voluntas* for the king's will was law; but both 'law' and 'will' must be reasonable and just: clause 4 of the charter demanded that a guardian should not during wardship take more from the land than was 'reasonable'. The Angevins, according to baronial opinion, had ruled unreasonably and unjustly, and rebellion was needed to restore the 'ancient usage' of Henry I. Were the barons fair in this opinion? Was the government of the Angevins, and particularly of King John, unjust and unreasonable? Or can it be argued that, after the loss of Normandy, John's presence in England and his extension of administration and justice were resented by a selfish baronage who preferred an absentee king like Richard? This is the crucial issue of the reign of King John.

ADMINISTRATION

Angevin administration was certainly extended by King John who seems to have taken a very personal interest in all aspects of law and government, especially after the loss of Normandy forced him into almost permanent residence in England (**23,** ch. 9). Saxon kings before 1066 had possessed certain rights as leaders of the people, such as military leadership and protection of the Witan or Council and the law courts. On top of these rights the Normans added feudal over-lordship and the concept of fealty: the king was, it is true, *primus inter pares*, he held the same rights of wardship and marriage, the same rights of holding a feudal court for his vassals as all other feudal lords. But as a feudal king he held two additional advantages: all justice derived from his court since other judges were merely delegated, and all land was held of him. The Angevins made law and administration more formalised and systematic, with fixed and set procedures based on writs obtained from the royal chancery. But, throughout, kingship was essentially personal: the king inherited his lands by the rules of family inheritance and in fact in the twelfth century much of the royal demesne was lost through gifts to barons for their support. Moreover, in the twelfth century the king's will was expressed orally and then confirmed by a writ or charter, but it was by the personal oral grant that it was dated. Indeed much of the royal administration was conducted by the king's own will, *voluntas* rather than by the law or state machinery: the word *rex* is derived from *recte*—the king had to rule justly for there was no distinction between personal morality and politics. The king derived his power from God, as John of Salisbury pointed out in the middle of the twelfth century, and though he was responsible for his subjects he was not responsible to them. Moreover, if he did act arbitrarily—and in the twelfth-century personal monarchy it was quite accepted that he would—and even if he acted tyrannically, there was no power to compel or constrain him. He was responsible to God, and also to the 'common counsel of the Realm' as the charter of Henry I indicated [**doc. 1**], though it was not until the thirteenth century that this became really meaningful. Hence he could rule legitimately through his own will as well as the law: this can be admirably illustrated by the cases of the bishop of Worcester who was deprived of his Gloucestershire fees for insulting a royal messenger, and Roger de Cressi, who married without the permission of a guardian appointed by John, and who had to pay 1,200 marks in 1207 *pro habenda benevolentia regis* and to recover his lands (**29**). Within the sphere of such personal government it was very difficult for the barons to define exactly what was *injuste*.

The feudal monarch ruled through his Household and an informal system of familiars, as well as the institutions of government like Chancery and Exchequer. This system of administration was fluid and open to continual change: as Professor Cheney has written, 'the personality of the office holder counted for more than the preconceived ideas of what duties went with which office' (**9**, p. 90). Quite often John created an office especially for a certain familiar, as the office of Keeper of the King's Ships and Ports, very important in the king's plans for the recovery of Normandy, was created for William of Wrotham. In addition important positions in local government and castles were given to the king's trusted advisers, such as Robert de Vieupont and Brian de Lisle (**23**, ch. 10), and the Close Rolls reveal a large number of grants of lands and money, not only to Household familiars like William de Harcourt, 'our seneschal', but also to foreign mercenaries such as Terry Teutonicus and Armando de Mongezir. Jolliffe, particularly, has seen the essence of John's administration in the personal contact of the king and his Household as emphasised, not only in the growth of the Chamber and Castle Treasures, but also in the position of seneschal, whose name appears between the barons and knights in the witness lists of royal charters and who replaced the constable as the paymaster of the Household (**29**). Not only was he responsible for organising all Household officials including the professional justices of the court *coram rege* and the Justices in Eyre, but he also organised the rebuilding of such castles as Woodstock, the royal hunting lodge. The butler, too, developed from being a Household official responsible for the king's wine, to a resident of Southampton from where he controlled the whole Gascon wine trade and was always consulted by the king about plans for expeditions to Poitou.

Thus the central government was conducted by the king himself through a system of Household officials, and the king's personal interest in government was greatly increased by the loss of Normandy. This is clearly indicated by the decline, during John's reign, of the power of the justiciar, the king's *alter ego*, a topic fully dealt with by F. W. West (**68**). During Richard's frequent absence from England the justiciar ruled in his stead: Hubert Walter, though he did not possess the official title, combined the official and military functions of kingship between 1193 and 1198. He had to act decisively to defeat Prince John's rebellion in 1194 by laying siege to Marlborough himself and by summoning a mixed council of barons and bishops to disseise John of all his English lands; further, a later clerical assembly threatened John with excommunication if he failed to make his peace with the king. Hubert issued articles for the 1194 eyres, he extracted an oath from all men over fifteen years of age that they would keep the peace and in 1197 he summoned all the great magnates of the realm to Oxford to agree to an aid for King Richard's wars. The justiciar was the first man in the realm in the king's absence but this situation ceased during John's reign, since after 1204 the king was only absent for any length of time in 1206 and 1214. West records how Geoffrey FitzPeter supplied John with treasure in Poitou in 1206 and performed essential administrative functions, including the receipt of homage, in the king's absence; in 1210 when John was in Ireland Geoffrey conducted the expedition against the Braose family in Wales. Similarly Peter des Roches helped in 1214 to tie up the details of John's submission to Rome and conducted routine administrative matters in the justiciar's name, using clerks from the royal Chancery: to pardon an outlaw or disseise an individual or his land involved letters to sheriffs and many others.

During the large part of the reign, however, the king himself was present and in full command: the Barons of the Exchequer now deferred problems to John himself, difficult or important cases now became the prerogative of the king in his court *coram rege* rather than of the justiciar and the Bench at Westminster. The court *coram rege* had its own justices and, although Geoffrey FitzPeter often sat in it, he played little part in its regular procedure and was not responsible for the issue of its final concords; his presence indeed was often necessary when a case from the Bench at Westminster was deferred to the king's court. Geoffrey's successor, moreover, was Peter des Roches, an ecclesiastic rather than a lawyer, who relied even more heavily on the legal experts of the court *coram rege*. After 1210 the Bench no longer sat at Westminster, but was wholly superseded by the court *coram rege*; it was restored temporarily during the king's absence in 1214 but only using royal justices like Richard Marsh and William Briwerre, and ceased again on the king's return, so that clause 17 of Magna Carta could appeal for a fixed court for the barons' convenience. Even in financial administration the justiciar was replaced by the king himself, when the Exchequer, of which Geoffrey FitzPeter was president, was ousted by the Household Chamber and Wardrobe, except in the annual audit of sheriffs' returns. Occasionally reference was made to Geoffrey for factual information but the usual procedure in the case of an Exchequer dispute was *loquendum cum rege*.

John was not only more personally involved in administration, he also made it more efficient, though much of this was the work of the chancellor Hubert Walter (**9**). The Chancery originated as part of the Household since the chancellor's function was to keep the King's Seal, so it was necessary that he should be available when needed by the king. Henry I also made his chancellor the head of the *scriptorium* or writing office, and Becket, chancellor from 1154 to 1162, used a permanent and trained staff of experts like Geoffrey Ridel and Nicholas of the Seal (**65**). During Richard's reign the symbol '*Teste me ipso*' was first used at the end of royal letters, though this is not evidence that the king read every one, and all charters were dated, since recipients were beginning to date grants from the date of the written charter not from the date of the oral grant as was previously the case; further Richard associated the office of chancellor with that of the justiciar, though in 1199 John immediately separated them again. It was his ordinance of that year that finally saw the emergence of the Chancery as a separate writing office; he ordered the registration of all royal and official letters in the Chancery, Praestita and Mise Rolls, thus increasing the efficiency of justice and administration which had formerly depended on the memory of officials and the retention of charters by their recipients. H. G. Richardson has argued that the original purpose of this ordinance was financial (**51**), though he has been severely criticised in this by Painter (**37**, pp. 100–2), who emphasises the official value of the Rolls. Moreover, now the Chancery was separate from the Exchequer, there was an increasing problem over the king's seal. The 'Dialogue of the Exchequer' (**28**) had distinguished in Henry II's reign between the 'royal seal in the Exchequer' and 'the royal seal which stays with the king', while during Richard's absence on crusade a deputy chancellor was left in England with the small seal. John certainly used the *parvum sigillum* for authorising private letters close, and on 10 May 1208 he used it at Tewkesbury because he did not have the Great Seal with him. Tout has indicated, moreover, that John used the small seal for chamber business, while continuing the use of the Great Seal on Exchequer business (**65**). Certainly as government institutions developed out of the royal household and took a much wider control over the country's affairs, John's administration became more complex. This was particularly true of financial administration, the increased efficiency of which affected John's subjects a great deal.

FINANCIAL ADMINISTRATION

The central organ of royal financial collection and record was the Exchequer, the procedure of which can be clearly seen from the 'Dialogue' (**28**): it was initially the occasion on which the treasurer came from Winchester to Westminster to receive and record sheriffs' accounts, including any writs of *computate* and *perdono*, to make and issue tallies, check the purity of the coinage and generally try to ensure that sheriffs were not defrauding the Crown. As well as their farms, sheriffs had to account their judicial profits, scutages and other extra payments, and town reeves, bailiffs and stewards were also present to account. The treasurer, and later the clerk of the Pipe, then wrote up the Pipe Roll to record the proceedings; after 1154 the series of Pipe Rolls is complete but before that date there is just one isolated roll extant, that of 1130. A typical early writ, of about 1116, runs as follows: 'Henry, king of the English, to Richard de Monte, greeting. Cause the abbot of Westminster to have 10/- of my alms as it is in my rolls. Witness the Bishop of Salisbury at Cannock, and this every year' (**43**). By such writs the king in person could direct the workings of his financial institutions through the use of local sheriffs who would then claim at their annual account at Westminster. Gradually too, the Exchequer became a court, initially merely a meeting for the court *coram rege* in the king's presence to deal with cases of finance and property; eventually the king was leaving such cases to the decision of the 'barons' of the Exchequer under their president the justiciar.

In John's reign the administration of the Exchequer was organised largely by Bishop William of Ely, who succeeded his kinsman, Bishop Richard, in 1199, and remained loyal to John throughout the interdict, for which he was rewarded with several manors and prebends (**103**). It seems that he was responsible for much of the improved neatness in financial procedure during the reign, thus enabling the king to put more efficient pressure on his barons. He began to state the amount due from each sheriff on the Pipe Roll at the head of each separate account; he began to use evidence from feet of fines at the Exchequer Court, and he may have been ultimately responsible for the system of feet of fines itself as well as the use of *tallia dividenda*. He even had a limited but sophisticated civil service, many of the clerks being housed near Westminster on a piece of land bought by William Maudit especially for the purpose; some of the clerks, moreover, were used by private citizens as attorneys in cases at the Exchequer.

The system did not always work smoothly in practice. The Memoranda Roll for 1199 (**51**), the special roll to record debts not paid, records that debts from the Devonshire farm for 1194–95 were still not paid in 1199, while in the roll for 1208 Hubert de Burgh was distrained for a long-standing debt of £31. There is no clear record that Hubert paid before 1216 and since he was high in the royal favour under Henry III the debt was never collected. In addition, the sheriff's farm was quite clearly less than the total of money he collected, so that Richard had charged seventeen of his sheriffs a *crementum*, an additional sum to account for the profit. John did likewise in 1205 and the increase was easily accepted by the sheriffs, though clause 25 of Magna Carta demanded the removal of the *crementum*, since it was thought that the sheriffs, who worked hard unpaid, deserved some profit. This was just one of the many increasingly complex factors in feudal finance which, because of delays and disputes, meant that the Memoranda Roll became the most important Exchequer document. The pressures of time and bulk had by 1199 made Henry II's system of accounting and auditing completely unworkable (**97**). It became increasingly impossible to collect all accounts into the Exchequer within the time laid down in the 'Dialogue' so that the audit became spread over a longer period and the whole working of the financial year was breaking down. John's Exchequer needed a permanent clerical staff as well as blank Pipe Rolls drawn up in advance on which accounts could be registered as they were paid. But even these developments were not enough to cope with the increasing pressure.

It was for this reason, and because it gave him easier access to his money, that John developed the use of the Chamber out of Household and Familiar administration (**93**) and also obtained loans from sheriffs which they could later recover from the Exchequer during their annual account. Before 1204 John's expenditure was based on two central treasuries, one at Winchester and the other at Caen in Normandy, and a regular series of 'wardrobe carts' was used to bring silver pennies from Winchester and Caen to the king wherever he happened to be. John certainly found this procedure slow and cumbersome and possibly expensive; moreover, in 1204 the Treasury at Caen was captured by Philip Augustus and so John had recourse to the ambulatory chamber as the office of all receipt and expenditure. When Normandy had been lost many clerks, who had served as paymasters of castles and supervisors of provisions, returned to England and were given office, some even being made joint-sheriffs to increase the exploitation of the counties, men like Robert FitzHermer in Buckinghamshire and Brian de Lisle who received Knaresborough castle in 1205. As John's familiars were placed in important offices, so receipt and expenditure became more involved with the Household than the Exchequer. Reginald of Cornhill and Stephen of Thurnham were used to hear the king's accounts in the Chamber, while Richard Marsh became *clericus camerae*, a financial official totally independent of the Exchequer. The Chamber was used to receive a number of John's financial measures: there is no mention on the Pipe Roll of the thirteenth of 1207, the tallage of 1210 or of the taxes on the Jews, so presumably the Chamber dealt with these, though there may have been a separate body for the Jews. It also handled profits from the interdict and feudal finance, especially money gained from wardships and reliefs, aids and custodies, for in John's reign this was one of the largest sources of income. Money formerly paid into the Exchequer could easily be commandeered for the Chamber: Chancery clerks would simply issue a writ of *liberate* or *computate* to the Exchequer, so that the Treasuer would know where the money had gone; similarly the

Chamber could notify the Exchequer of fines made by individuals with the king *pro benevolentia regis*. Gradually, because of its convenience and ease of operation, the Chamber became the personal instrument by which the king could receive money, though its records were by no means as efficient as those of the Exchequer.

Moreover, the king decided, after the loss of Caen, that one or two central treasuries could be both cumbersome and costly; hence in 1207 he transported 11,000 marks from Winchester to Nottingham and in the following year 17,000 marks from Westminster to Bristol. He began generally to deposit ready supplies of cash in castle keeps throughout the country to be on tap whenever he was in need. Jolliffe, in fact, sees these castle treasuries as the symbol of John's financial decentralisation (**93**) and it certainly helped the king on several occasions: in 1212 he used Nottingham as a source of supply in planning the abortive Welsh campaign and in 1214 he transported money from both Nottingham and Bristol for the Poitevin campaign. His immediate concern in October 1214 on his return from Poitou was to restock his castles, and it could be argued that John's poverty was one of the reasons for his failure to take direct action against baronial conspirators in 1214–15. Certainly John had to fall back on the Exchequer to pay his mercenaries in 1215, and during the civil war he rewarded them by gifts of captured territory until, by his death, he was again rebuilding the stocks in his castles. Now it is important to realise that castle treasuries were not new (**71**): Henry II had used Southampton and Exeter for the purpose. What was new under John, however, was their control by the Chamber and the bypassing of the Exchequer in the transfer of money authorised solely by *clerici camerae*.

One important household official who well illustrates the growth of castle treasuries and their connection with the Chamber is Philip Mark at Nottingham (**83**). Situated in a crucial position for the north of England and North Wales, Nottinghamshire was a county of prolific escheats and a large area of royal demesne, as well as much royal forest and the Clipstone hunting lodge. Hence John often used it as a centre for account, and after 1209, when Philip Mark became castellan, as his base for expeditions to Wales or the north. In 1210 the scutage for Ireland from Yorkshire and Northumberland was collected there, and during the civil war it remained the only royal outpost in the area and was consequently quickly drained of its cash.

It has already been shown that, in addition to the Chamber, John could also use his sheriffs as sources of the ready supply of cash (**29**). Reginald of Cornhill, the sheriff of Kent, should have accounted for over £8,000 to the Exchequer in 1205, but of this he in fact paid only £15, the rest having been commandeered earlier in the year by King John's writ. The king made similar use of William of Wrotham, the Keeper of the King's Ports, who was made controller of the fifteenth levied on French merchants and allowed to collect the tax. William had, in fact, a long history of financial connection with the Crown: in 1205 he was keeper of the revenues of the see of Winchester and in the following year he added those of Bath too. From the revenues of these he obviously acted as paymaster for the fleet that sailed with John to Poitou in 1206, for on 8 June 1205 a writ *computate* was issued in his favour for £130 10s 0d, and a writ *liberate* for £340 and further sums were paid to him in 1206 when the expedition did in fact sail. All naval matters, it seems, were under his financial control and the king allowed him his expenses from his accounts to the Exchequer (**70**). Thus, from all these measures, John had more ready cash more easily available, which was important initially for his plans to recover Normandy and later to control the baronial and Welsh conspiracies.

Other changes were made in financial administration during the reign which also increased efficiency. While the cost of government had increased considerably since Henry II's reign, the amount paid by the sheriffs in their farms had remained steady, apart from an increment imposed by Richard; John also in 1205 added an increment and insisted that it be accounted separately. Moreover, he dismissed all his sheriffs and reappointed them in selected shires as custodians; this meant that the custodian, like the guardian of a feudal wardship, had to account for his income and expenditure, item by item, an attempt by the king to realise for himself the full value of a shire (**82**). Further, he often allowed sheriffs to fine for their increments, so that in 1208 Hubert de Burgh, for instance, could offer a fine of £100 to be quit of an increment of £400. Thus John was at least certain of the £100 in cash immediately. Often too, a sheriff could buy a farm by offering to pay the full increment: Thomas of Moreton offered a £200 increment if he could be sheriff of Lincolnshire in 1205. Custodies in fact became a common feature of the reign: in 1208 the king paid John of Conard a sum of £20 a year provided John accounted for Otford castle as a custody rather than as a farm, and by 1209 only four sheriffs were still accounting for farms, the rest being regarded as custodians so that clause 25 of Magna Carta could demand that 'all shires shall be at the ancient farm, without any increment'.

To streamline procedure within the Exchequer the idea of *tallia dividenda* was introduced (97). Henry II's reforms had meant that sheriffs were having to cope with a large number of increasingly complex fines; for instance, on the Pipe Roll of 1200 the sheriff of Yorkshire owed £610 paid by 1,094 debtors, so that the Exchequer would need to match up 1,094 tallies when the debts were paid. In 1206, therefore, the idea was developed of giving the sheriff just one tally to cover all the debts of his shire. This relieved congestion in both the Pipe Roll, where the name of the sheriff only was recorded, and the Upper Exchequer of Receipt, so that by the fourteenth century the whole process of collecting fines had been decentralised, with the sheriff coming between the central authority and the local debtor.

In addition, John tried to preserve the value of the English coinage. The Waverley Annals record great disturbances in England in 1203 *per tonsuram sterlingorum*, and several other chroniclers mention that clipping coins was reducing the value of the coinage. As a result John wrote to all sheriffs on 9 November 1204 that no one was to possess clipped coins after 13 January 1205, the punishment for offenders being the confiscation of their lands. Further the sheriff was to appoint four worthy men for each town where a market was held to carry out the king's command. By the Assize of 26 January 1205 anyone caught in possession of new clipped coins was to be accused of theft: it is interesting to note that several Jews fined with the king to be quit of this offence. In addition John gained considerable sums of money by farming out local exchanges and mints, of which there were eight. The king was using every opportunity, ably supported by William of Ely, to streamline English financial procedure, both for his own advantage and in the public interest. This can be seen very clearly in William's improvements in financial records (91): in addition to the Memoranda Roll, a procedure of *communia* at the Exchequer was developed, mostly *Dies Dati*, whereby each baron and sheriff received notification of the exact day he had to account and each entry had its county in the margin for easy reference. Further the Exchequer began to use county membranes, on which was recorded any matter left unsettled by each shire account, and which was closely related to the actual Pipe Roll where a blank space was left for '*debet*' in cases where the full amount had not been paid. The Memoranda Roll was subdivided with a separate membrane for the Jews so that, together with Charter Rolls, like Fine and Prest Rolls, the king must have been able to squeeze exactly what was owed from his barons. It was his increasing efficiency in financial administration which put pressure on them, together with their inability after 1204 to gain remission on their debts by service in Normandy (**23,** p. 150).

THE KING'S INCOME

Frank Barlow (**1,** p. 402) has assessed John's financial problem thus: 'All taxation was detested unless its purpose was obvious and popular. And John's purposes were seldom popular in England. The English baronage as a whole quickly lost interest in the recovery of the king's continental demesne and grudged the cost. It also feared lest John should become too strong.' In considering how far John's government was oppressive, historians have concentrated much of their attention on taxation and financial exactions: Jolliffe (**29**), for instance, has emphasised the personal nature of the monarchy, so that subjects even had to fine for the king's *benevolentia* or good will. The scramble for favour, inherent in the system of patronage which was at the base of twelfth-century government, is witnessed in the Fine Rolls: 'Roger, son of Nicholas, offers several lampreys if the king will induce William Marshal to grant him the manor of Longford' (quoted in **42**). Barons were prepared to pay for the royal favour and good will, expressed in the form of a wardship or a marriage to a wealthy heiress; they knew their debts might never be paid because of the difficulty of collection, the leniency of officials, the eagerness of the government to accept a smaller cash payment in lieu of a full payment which might be difficult to collect, and finally because of the system of instalments, by which barons usually repaid debts to the king. Thomas de Erdington offered 5,000 marks in 1215 for the custody of a barony but the instalments were so small during Henry III's reign, when Thomas was in the king's favour, that the debt would have been finally repaid by 1917. Again, of John de Lacy's relief of 7,000 marks only 2,000 marks was paid while the rest was forgiven in 1214 when the king was desperate for the support of the constable of Chester. Indeed this served the king's political advantage, for an unpaid debt would ensure loyalty in the hope of some remission of the debt: in 1213, for instance, John promised to cancel all Exchequer debts for those who served overseas for a year. Indeed so much of the financial system of feudal government worked as much to the barons' advantage as to the king's, particularly the feudal incidents, relief, wardship and marriage.

Henry I's Coronation Charter had promised that reliefs should be 'just and reasonable' [**doc. 1**], but throughout the twelfth century this definition was not strict enough. Glanville and the Dialogue both fixed the relief for a knight's fee at 100s and by and large Henry II kept to that figure. The knight's fee varied little in size, whereas the barony varied from one to hundreds of knights' fees: what, then, was to be the relief for a barony? By custom it was £100, but Henry II had charged Robert de Lacy 1,000 marks in 1178 and Walter Brito had paid £200 in 1166 for a barony which comprised just fifteen knights' fees. John also exceeded the 'reasonable' limit for reliefs, though he was sometimes content with the traditional £100, as when John de Balon paid for a barony consisting of just one knight's fee in 1203. John de Lacy had to pay 7,000 marks to succeed his father as constable of Chester, while William FitzAlan had to pay 10,000 marks in 1214, so that Painter has concluded: 'All in all there seems to be no doubt whatever that John charged exorbitant reliefs throughout his reign and that some of those imposed in 1212 and 1214 can only be described as fantastic' (**37**, p. 221).

John's use of wardship and marriage appears to have been similarly 'unreasonable'. A young heir, incapable of rendering the feudal services to his lord and king, was forced instead to yield the profits of his estates to a guardian appointed by the king. An heiress or widow must marry with the king's approval or one of the king's enemies might control her land. Yet these basic principles, accepted by feudal custom, were stretched to their legal limit by the Angevins, who were prepared to use force and distraint to get their way: in 1205 John confiscated the lands of Alice Belet because she refused to marry Ralph Ridel as John had asked. Such widows feared social disparagement by a marriage to one of the king's familiars or foreign mercenaries, since this was a useful method for the king to reward his servants. Margery, the widow of Robert FitzRoger, had therefore to pay the king £1000 for the right to choose her own husband and retain her inheritance; the countess of Aumale had to pay 5,000 marks for the same privileges. Alternatively the king secured cash from those who wanted heiresses, such men as Geoffrey de Mandeville who paid the totally unprecedented sum of 20,000 marks for Isabella of Gloucester, though it must be admitted that, as the king's ex-wife, she was a very valuable match. On some occasions widows were even auctioned to the highest bidder, and the estates of wards were often cruelly mismanaged in an attempt to make them yield the highest profit before the heir came of age; in addition, through John's development of prerogative wardship, he claimed custody not only of the fiefs held directly of him by his tenants in chief but also of all other fiefs held by the same tenants. Thus, although a baron might hold just one knight's fee from the king and hundreds from other lords, the whole barony came into the king's custody during wardship (**37,** p. 216). It is, however, particularly difficult to examine accurately the barons' grievances over wardship because of lack of evidence, though their opposition to John's extreme pressure on feudal incidents can be seen from the details of the Charter itself.

Similar to feudal incidents was the gracious aid levied, with baronial consent, on just three occasions, the marriage of the king's daughter, the knighting of his eldest son and the ransoming of his own person. The Angevins had requested aids on a variety of occasions such as crusades or foreign wars, and John in 1210 levied an aid on Bristol and Gloucester to pay for his passage to Ireland (**37,** p. 215). The essential feudal levy was, however, military service itself. Mitchell has shown that to hire a mercenary knight in John's reign cost 2*s* per day in contrast to 8*d* per day under Henry II; thus for forty days one knight would cost £4. On average, however, a tenant who paid scutage, instead of fighting in person, paid just £1 per knight's fee (**34**). Thus it was very important for John, whenever possible, to get actual service not scutage; but the calculation of service due was often difficult for quite often the *servitium debitum* did not correspond to the number of knights' fees which a baron held. Moreover, tenants in chief sometimes served with fractional quotas and paid cash for the remainder, so that gradually the fractional quota became accepted as the *servitium debitum*. Thus the barons could easily defraud the king of the service due: in 1205 about 4,000 tenants purchased exemption from the expedition to Poitou, while in 1213 the expedition was prevented by the barons' refusal to pay or serve. Even in Poitou itself John could not trust the service of the magnates, as illustrated by his retreat from La Roche aux Moins in 1214. For continental service, forty days was not long enough, so the king was prepared to accept a cash substitute in 1205 even though it was to his own disadvantage. Clearly the barons benefited from this financially, even more so since they were finding it difficult to enforce the due service from their subtenants, and since many holdings were of just half or one-third of a knight's fee; further since there was no legal service beyond forty days the barons were unwilling to surrender the whole summer away from their estates: the Close Rolls for 1212 reveal that the Abbey of Ramsey sent four knights to Wales and ordered the rest to pay cash so that the four could serve for a period longer than forty days, while Geoffrey de Neville was given cash by the king to pay his knights if the period of service exceeded forty days. It seems therefore that the king was aware of the problems posed by military service: the barons had no justification for their refusal in 1213.

Scutage was a cash payment in lieu of service, usual at the rate of £1 per knight's fee; it was owed like the service itself so it did not need baronial consent. But John exceeded his rights over scutage: he levied eleven scutages compared with Richard's three and Henry II's eight, and on two occasions he raised the rate to £2. In 1209 he imposed a scutage against the Scots, even though a treaty was signed at Norham and no campaign fought. Two years later he summoned the knights of Eustace de Vesci and Robert FitzWalter and the subtenants of the exiled bishops, and sent one hundred knights to France, compelling the others to fine for exemption at the rate of 10 marks per fee. In addition, since most barons made a profit by paying scutage rather than serving in person, John followed his brother's practice of fining those who paid scutage an extra sum on top of the scutage. By 1210 this extra fine was 10 marks per knight's fee (**37**, p. 128). The result of this measure was baronial hostility, since it was difficult for barons to collect in full from their subtenants, and also the hostility of knights who were being squeezed by their barons to pay their share. All blamed the king. There was no justification, however, for the demand of clause 12 of Magna Carta that scutage, like an aid, should be levied only by the 'common consent of our kingdom'. Again the barons were demanding more than that to which they were legally entitled.

Monasteries which held land by military service could either pay scutage or a fine in a lump sum, a *donum*, for exemption from service; any monastery which held land on terms other than military service would be asked by the king to pay a *donum* or *auxilium* on the occasions when military tenants paid scutage. The only other important group not involved in military service consisted of the cities and boroughs of the royal demesne: these paid the tallage, not necessarily on the occasions when scutage was demanded but rather when the feudal tenants paid an aid. The amount of tallage varied and was increased by John: London paid 1,500 marks in 1204 but 2,000 marks in 1210 and 1214; Cambridge paid 60 marks and then 150 marks in 1210 and 1214. Taken together scutages, fines, tallages and *dona* yielded 25,000 marks in 1210, one of the heaviest years, but even this figure fell below John's needs. His difficulty was that, with the expense of recovering Normandy and the increased cost of government, he had to fall back either on new methods of taxation or on increasing the rate and frequency of old methods like scutage. It may have been the latter that aroused baronial hostility, but it was the former which, according to Mitchell, was the basis of modern taxation (**34**). These new methods had their origin in the gracious aids, a general tax levied for the needs of the government on all those in the government's care. A carucage was an 'aid from ploughs' or 'pennies assessed on ploughs for the king's aid'; it was assessed just once in John's reign, to pay the relief of 20,000 marks to Philip Augustus in 1200. Evidence suggests it was difficult to assess and collect but Painter estimates a possible yield of about £7,500 (**37,** p. 129).

The most fruitful type of aid for John was the tax on movables. The Saladin tithe on movables and revenues of 1188 and the one-fourth levied in 1193 for the king's ransom both yielded huge sums. Wendover records that John tried a levy on movables on the barons in 1203, and there is other evidence to show that this may have been a general levy, but we have no idea of how much it produced. Four years later, after the vast expense of the 1206 campaign, John summoned the barons to a Council at Oxford where a general levy of one-thirteenth of revenues and movables was agreed 'by the common consent of our Council at Oxford for the defence of our realm and the recovery of our rights'. Writs were issued to the whole realm: 'All seneschals and bailiffs of earls and barons shall swear openly before my justices concerning the value of their lord's and their own rents and movable chattels, and every man other than earls and barons shall swear concerning their own.' The punishment for those who defrauded the justices was imprisonment or confiscation. Some did try, but were discovered: Ruald FitzAlan lost Richmond castle on 27 May for refusing to swear to the value of his goods and chattels. Many concealed their goods in monasteries, especially Cistercian houses, since the tax collectors had no need to visit them, but a writ of 16 April ordered all religious in Lincolnshire to surrender any goods deposited with them. Mitchell has seen the thirteenth of 1207 as early modern taxation, since it was not a feudal aid but rather an aid to carry on a war in the future. It was levied on the property and goods of all classes, its assessment and collection were national not feudal using travelling justices and royal officials rather than feudal tenants; moreover, the unit of the levy was the vill not the knight's fee. Painter estimates the total yield of the tax at about £60,000, a colossal sum (**37,** p. 135), but its unpopularity rested more on the principle of non-feudal all-embracing taxation. Although it needed, like all aids, baronial consent, and although John did not use it a second time, it could give the king increasing control over taxation.

Another important area of non-feudal taxation was the king's regalian rights over the Church (**25**). During any episcopal vacancy the king could use the revenues of the see for his own purpose and present clerks to benefices as he wished; further, while the lands were considered part of the king's demesne he could levy a tallage on them. While there is no evidence for increasingly heavy exactions during the interdict, John certainly made use of his regalian rights: the Canterbury tallage of 1206 yielded over £1,000 while the Lincoln vacancy produced nearly £2,000 in one and half years in 1207-8. Some of these increases can be explained by direct exploitation of the estates and the overall expansion of the economy during John's reign. Yet, on the other hand, the historian must do justice to John's financial expertise: between 1199 and 1207 he levied five tallages on vacant sees but from 1207 to 1216 only two. These two, however, were much heavier in their demands and in addition John developed the new principle, that every bishopric should be tallaged at least once during a vacancy, whether there was a general tallage or not. Durham was tallaged in 1208 and Exeter in 1211 though there was no general tallage during those years; further the bishoprics yielded more, for Durham paid £1,154 in 1208 compared to £341 in 1196.

Probably one of the most profitable sources of income for all the Angevins, and particularly King John, was the Jews. Wendover records that in 1210 John ordered that throughout the whole realm Jews of both sexes be imprisoned and severely tortured so that they would fine for the king's good will. As a result several were so severely tortured that they gave the king all that they had and promised more to evade such great torments. Among these was a Bristol Jew who, although tortured, refused to fine with the king to recover his freedom; the king therefore ordered his torturers that each day one of his teeth should be pulled out until he agreed to pay the king 10,000 marks of silver. After seven days, seven teeth had been extracted giving the Jew intolerable pain and on the eighth day the torturers were beginning to extract the eighth tooth when the Jew relented and offered to pay the said sum so that he might save his eighth tooth.

John, however, was more subtle than this mythical tale would allow. Henry II and Richard had been remarkably moderate in their demands from the Jews, the latter exacting just four contributions for a total of about 10,000 marks. John, however, demanded 4,000 marks for confirming their Charters of Privilege in 1200; in 1205 he requested a *promissum* of bezants and two years later a tallage of 4,000 marks. In the same year a tax of one-tenth of Jewish income was levied and it was because he thought that many Jews had evaded the tax that John ordered their imprisonment in 1210. In 1209 every Jew had been requested to furnish to the king a list of all the debts he was owed; many had apparently concealed their credits and hence Wendover's dramatic tale, the results of which according to the Waverley Annals yielded 66,000 marks. In the following year the chattels of several Jews were sold and the profits given to the king; some like Isaac of Norwich fined with the king for his good will, but others like Isaac of Canterbury were hanged and their houses sold. Further, although John preferred to borrow money from Christian merchants, Flemings, Lombards and Catalans, when a Jew died the Crown took over his bonds and the loan had to be repaid to the Crown or a fine made for the debtor to be quit. Finally, though it should not receive too much emphasis until the middle of the thirteenth century, John's development of Jewish administration, with special justices and Jewish Exchequer, did allow more efficient collection of debts and taxing of the Jews.

If taxes on the Jews yielded the king most money, taxes on the forest yielded most bitterness. Richard's heavy forest eyre of 1198 had driven many to buy privileges or exemptions from forest exactions by 1204. John's eyre of 1207 was equally heavy, assessing amercements at £1,300 in Yorkshire alone and resulting, according to Wendover, in the king's destruction of all hedges and ditches in royal forests. Moreover, according to Coventry, John began a second, even more searching, forest eyre in 1212 when Yorkshire's amercements amounted to £1,250. The significant reason for baronial opposition to these exactions was that the forest was the king's prerogative; as Holt has shown, 'its law derived solely from the king's will and bore no relation to the custom of the realm' (**23,** pp. 158, 159). Moreover, forest rules affected local landowners seriously by preventing any expansion of their arable, so any illegal extensions discovered by the two forest eyres must have been severely resented by the barons.

In addition John derived much revenue from trade: he made profitable experiments of one-fifteenth on all imports and exports, but had to stop when the truce with Philip Augustus in 1206 involved free trade. However, the use of custodians at ports, the division of the coastline into districts for easier supervision and the royal control of monopolies all yielded valuable revenue, without arousing hostility from the politically powerful sections of the community.

JUSTICE

The prime function of the medieval monarch was to give good law and justice to his people. Henry I in his coronation oath promised to abolish all the 'evil practices' of his brother's reign and guarantee good justice instead [**doc. 1**]. Did John depart from this view? Was it arbitrary behaviour by the king and his justices that caused clauses 17, 20, 34, 39 and 40 of Magna Carta [**doc. 20**]? The Charter was an appeal for good customary law, which the barons felt that the Angevins had abandoned; it was, moreover, the king's law since all justice came from the royal court as a prerogative which kings allowed their subjects to share. There was no independent judiciary, but although the king defined law and was not responsible to it, he was expected to rule 'reasonably' and to further the growth of good law for the benefit of his subjects. It was in reconciling these two principles that the barons faced one of their most difficult problems.

How interested was King John in giving good justice? Lady

Stenton has argued his own personal involvement in the judicial administration of the country, for even during the civil war of 1216 he appointed four men to hear disputes at Northampton (**108**). She emphasises his concern for customary law—'Do nothing', he wrote to the justiciar in 1203, 'contrary to the customs of our kingdom' —his tours around the country accompanied by justices and justiciar, the increased volume of business to come before the royal courts and the failure of the Justices in Eyre to keep their timetables. Many cases, indeed, were of such magnitude that they had to be settled by the king himself: the quarrel between the Earl of Chester and the Advocate of Bethune had to be decided by the king and 'the king wishes to do to each as he ought'. Finally she emphasises the decline in the power of the Bench, the fixed court at Westminster under the justiciar, and the corresponding rise of the court *coram rege*, the king's own ambulatory court, under his specialist judges like Simon of Pattishall and James of Potterne, fully expert in the English legal system. By 1208 there were only three justices at Westminer, and by 1209 the Bench had ceased to exist altogether, though it does seem that John wanted to keep it as a clearing house for cases. To Lady Stenton, therefore, the king was justice; from his interest it flowed throughout the realm.

This may be an exaggeration of the case. The decline of the Bench at Westminster had causes other than the rise of the court *coram rege*. Jenkinson has shown how the Exchequer's financial interest was expanding at such a rate in the twelfth century that it could no longer spare judges for the permanent judicial court at Westminster (**91**). Moreover, we shall later point out that it was administrative convenience that caused the growth of the court *coram rege*. Further John's tours were for an administrative and political purpose rather than a judicial one: as Louis VI had continually patrolled his demesne in France, so John had to ensure his succession and then later the security of his country by progresses. This was a common feature of medieval monarchy; the king's court would be an added political support, especially as local magnates feared for their privileges and lesser people feared amercements. This, however, hardly indicates that the king was the motivating force of all justice. Just as Walter Map describes Henry II as a 'husband who is the last to hear of the unfaithfulness of his wife', so it is unlikely that John heard all cases in the court *coram rege*. Professor Cheney has asked 'Did King John normally hear the lawsuits in his court or did he, like his father,

leave them to his courtiers and go hunting? What did the letters
which went out from Rome in the name of Innocent III owe to the
personal initiative of the Pope? These problems deny certain
solutions; historians must content themselves with approximations'
(**9,** p. 91). The same question can be asked about the justiciar.
Geoffrey FitzPeter was, like Hubert Walter, a lawyer-administrator,
but it was physically impossible for him to perform all the tasks for
which he was theoretically responsible. Although master of the
Exchequer Court, he was not always present; although president of
the bench in final concords, he did not always attend cases; although
chief of the king's judges, he did not attend many sessions of the
court *coram rege*. There had developed a set procedure for justice
during the absence of the Angevin kings: innovations were carried
out, not necessarily through the king's initiative, and often in the
king's absence, just as Hubert Walter and William of Ely were
responsible for innovations in Chancery and Exchequer procedure.
Moreover, it was not the presence of the king or his justiciar that
litigants sought in the royal court: it was the prestige and finality of a
decision there. Undoubtedly the king's personal interest in justice
can be exaggerated.

Thus while the king was in theory the head of all justice, there was
a certain set procedure which royal justice followed. The reforms of
Henry II had depended on three principles: the system of writs
purchased from the king's Chancery to initiate an action in the
king's court; the Grand and Possessory Assizes as the basis of
particular civil actions; and the jury system. Moreover, these were
three types of court, all deriving their power from the king: the Bench
was resident at Westminster under the justiciar and was necessary
because of the king's frequent absence abroad. Justice also followed
the king's person, a completely informal court with no records and
no set procedure; after the loss of Normandy it became permanent in
England as the court *coram rege*. Finally justices were sent from the
king's court on circuits, or eyres, to a particular county to conduct
pleas of the Crown to save civil litigants the trouble and expense of a
journey to London or pursuit of the king's ambulatory court (**57,**
58). In these three courts much of the procedure was still informal
depending on the king or justiciar: in 1201 when John decided the
case between the earl of Chester and the advocate of Béthune there
was no record made of the decision in the Curia Regis Rolls. Moreover, cases were often postponed at the king's will, or, in his absence,

to await his decision. Geoffrey FitzPeter postponed three cases in Easter 1204 to await the king's return, perhaps because royal patronage or a large fine was involved, perhaps because the cases concerned important political figures. On the other hand, such informality and personal interference were being replaced by set procedure. Justices were becoming expert in the law and there was a growth in the number of literate laymen. Barons were required to adopt similar set procedures in their own feudal courts and so probably knew the law well themselves. Moreover, once a particular writ had been issued for a particular case, it followed the correct procedure until its conclusion (**1**, p. 317). Historians have argued that clause 40 of Magna Carta was a triumph for the king's justice: the barons did not want to pay extortionate prices for writs and did not want delays. They recognised the procedure as good and wanted more not less of it.

The growth of the Bench as a permanent offshoot of the king's Curia, resident at Westminster, occurred as a result of the Angevins' frequent absences abroad. Sitting under professional justices like Hubert Walter and Geoffrey FitzPeter, it was attached to the Exchequer and frequent overlaps occurred between the two, both in staffing and records. There was no distinction between the business of the Bench and the judicial function of the Curia that travelled to Normandy with the king, so that after 1204 it was unnecessary to have two courts in England. Moreover, with the king's permanent residence in England, the Household recovered its importance, the Chamber took financial business from the Exchequer and the court *coram rege* took judicial business from the Bench. Westminster did, however, retain much of its importance, for in 1206, 1210 and 1214 the king went on lengthy foreign expeditions, restoring the Justiciar and the Bench to their former position, and even when the king was in England, Geoffrey FitzPeter still discharged his judicial duties by his own writ: he continued to summon litigants to trial and appoint attorneys and days for particular cases. By 1209, however, his judicial function had declined, for in his own household John kept many learned justices whom he would use on the spot or despatch on particular circuits, while at Westminster, on the other hand, there was difficulty in recruiting enough justices (**68, 107, 108**). When the general eyre of 1208 was in process, the Bench had to be closed temporarily because its justices were needed for the eyre; further, since all the king's justices were at Northampton in 1209, the

Michaelmas session of the Bench was held there in the presence of both king and justiciar. After 1209 the Bench did not return to Westminster but became amalgamated with the court *coram rege*; indeed in John's absence of 1214, although the Bench returned to Westminster, it was really a session of the court *coram rege* conducted by the king's justices without the justiciar Peter des Roches who was not a lawyer. Thus, administrative reasons caused the decline of the Bench: it was not a plan by the king to control justice more fully himself. In fact, although more convenient for John, the court *coram rege* was less convenient for the barons, since the expense and delay of pursuing the ambulatory king were too heavy. Under Henry III, therefore, the Bench returned to Westminster, partly as a result of clause 17 of the Charter, partly because the young king was unable to conduct the court *coram rege* himself.

In addition to the two central courts, there was need for professional justices, both criminal and civil, to deal with local problems. These were provided by eyres, or itinerant justices' routes, instituted by Henry II at the Assize of Clarendon. Most of our knowledge of the eyres under John is gained from a survey of the Assize Rolls and the feet of fines, which are crucial for understanding the extent of the king's influence in local affairs and also for appreciating certain clauses of the Charter. The eyres certainly intrude the king's justice on the counties in a manner relatively efficient for the twelfth century. Lady Stenton has suggested, for instance, that the 1202 Northamptonshire eyre may have been part of a four-year cycle since there were eyres in that county in 1194 and 1198 as well, and in between justices did visit the county to cope with pressing judicial business, such as hearing adjourned cases, delivering jails and tallaging towns (**108**). The procedure adopted by the eyre ran as follows: criminal cases were registered under the Hundred in which the crime occurred and twelve jurors from each Hundred were summoned to appear before the justices. They were questioned on their local knowledge of the crimes and their answers had to agree with those drawn up by the sheriff and coroner. If the answers did not agree, the jurors could be fined. They were also required to answer more general questions on local markets, taxes and wardships. The justices then declared guilt or innocence and passed sentence; often, however, the verdict depended on the frank-pledge system, the support of the accused by his neighbours, trial by ordeal or some other appeal to divine judgment. How efficient was this system? Did it impress the fairness and justice and impartiality of the king's court on the king's subjects in the counties?

Certainly the eyres, if efficient by twelfth-century standards, were unreliable. They were rarely planned in detail beforehand for delays would always change any itinerary: in 1221 writs were sent to the sheriffs of the western counties about the forthcoming eyre, yet only the sheriff of Worcester, the first to be visited, could be given a date. Further, in 1202 at Lincoln the justices made no fines from mid-August to mid-September, perhaps because of illness or vacation. To make up such delays, the two justices often had to hold separate courts, in Lincolnshire *coram Eustace* and *coram Simon*. Delays were often caused too by essoins, excuses by litigants for non-attendance, usually because of illness or absence in the service of the king. They needed only a clerk to pass them and so could easily postpone a case. As a result cases from Bedford, Coventry and Leicester which had been delayed in the cause of the eyre were all tried at Northampton in August 1202, and on 15 September all *residua placitorum* were tried in the same hall at Lincoln, the hall being divided into three spaces for justices to deal with pleas of the crown and civil pleas, and a clerk to hear essoins. Moreover, men could evade the justice of the Crown, especially by recourse to the Church: the thorny problems of criminous clerks and sanctuary, as well as the luck of divine judgment at the ordeal, helped many evaders of the law, as indeed did the possibility of fleeing to the 'Greenwood' and becoming outlawed. The relative difficulty of communication and the corruption of local officials meant that capture and conviction were not always certain. Finally, too much depended on the personality of the justices, their memory and their knowledge of the law. The Assize Rolls which they compiled were handed over to the treasurer on their return, for copying up and filing at Westminster; their own copies were then destroyed. Any future reference to the cases conducted would then be made to the justices' memories rather than to the written record. All these factors helped to provide safety valves for English litigants. John could do nothing to prevent them.

The basic weakness, indeed, of the judicial system was revealed by the large number of amercements which John levied. The amercement was a fine on an individual who made a mistake in judicial procedure, perhaps by accusing a man found to be innocent, or by failing to serve as a juror when requested; it was not a punishment for a crime committed, though it might occasionally be this for a minor offence (**42**). The majority of cases that came before John's justices were solved in this way and, as a result, the coming of the county eyre was hated by all. In 1201–2 at Lincoln there were on record 114 murders, 89 crimes of violence and many other lesser crimes; of the criminals, two were hanged, sixteen outlawed and twenty-eight claimed sanctuary, benefit of clergy or the ordeal. The remaining 157 cases were dealt with by amercements. It was rarely the guilty party that was amerced for many remained undetected. Rather was it a local official or the local community that was amerced because they failed to produce the criminal. The system was fostered by frank-pledge, whereby each man joined a group of ten or twelve men and if one of their number was known to have committed a crime the rest were required to produce him. If they failed they were amerced. The fines were arbitrarily fixed, but at Lincoln in 1202 they yielded £633 15s 0d, of which £95 was paid by groups in frank-pledge (**57**). In civil cases, too, if a man was wronged and started a case by securing the king's writ, he was amerced if he finally yielded or carried it through without sufficient evidence to gain a conviction. Yet it was not the system that the barons objected to in clause 20 of the Charter; it was John's use of it to fill his coffers, his use of justice as a financial benefit [**doc. 20**]. Men were to be amerced according to the measure of the offence and their own ability to pay. The barons accepted the system but they resented John's use of it to his own advantage.

Was John's justice oppressive then? Historians have pointed to the demands embodied in the Charter as evidence of John's tyrannical behaviour: McKechnie (**32**) has referred to the increasing cost of writs to initiate judicial proceedings (cl. 40), the baronial fear of arbitrary imprisonment without judgment (cl. 39), the heavy amercements for *benevolentia regis* (cl. 20) and the expense and delay of justice from an ambulatory court (cl. 17), as well as their refusal to be robbed of their right to decide in their own courts all property cases between their feudal tenants (cl. 34). Recent research, however, has removed much of this vilification of John: Miss Hurnard has shown that clause 34 was not a denial of the barons' feudal rights of justice (**90**); F. W. West has emphasised that the cessation of the permanent Bench at Westminster was for judicial and administrative convenience and that ultimately John wanted a permanent court to work in conjunction with his ambulatory one (**68**). He certainly did overcharge his subjects for his law, though this was fair since law was regarded as the king's prerogative, not yet as a public right. Yet now that Normandy had been lost, and with it the safety valves of overseas campaigns and an absentee king, the pressure of John's tours, the increasing efficiency of his judicial reforms, and the obvious financial effects of these on the barons made life difficult for his subjects. Twelfth-century monarchs were allowed to be arbitrary; John, as Lady Stenton has shown, may have been more interested in government and justice than his otherwise preoccupied predecessors, and was therefore more arbitrary. It is difficult to accept the chroniclers' picture of him as a tyrant.

MILITARY ORGANISATION

Was John militarily weak? What sources of military power did he have in England and on the Continent? Did such military failures as the loss of Normandy and his inability to recover it in 1206 and 1214 arouse the hostility and contempt of the barons? How much did his own army depend on paid mercenary troops and leaders? What military grievances caused the barons to unite against their king? In an age, typified by Richard the Lionheart, in which military glory and power secured the support of a king's tenants in chief these questions are particularly relevant since John was undoubtedly a poor commander (**41**). It would be fascinating to know in more detail the effects of the surrender of Vaudreuil in 1203 by Robert FitzWalter and Saer de Quenci on their later relations with the king; it would be equally interesting to survey the numbers and extent of John's mercenaries during his preparations for war in 1215, the offices they held and their effects on the local barons. Finally, it would be useful to see how the 'Army of God' organised itself under Robert FitzWalter both before the Charter and during the civil war, and what resources it had. Many such questions must unfortunately remain unanswered in detail; but a survey of the organisation of John's army will give valuable insight into his own power and the reasons for baronial hostility.

The Angevin kings gave knights' fees to their tenants in chief on condition that each promised to support them with so many knights, the *servitium debitum* fixed by the *Cartae Baronum* of 1166, armed and mounted for a period of forty days. There were, however, several practical difficulties in this system. The forty-day limit was much too short for most campaigns, especially those in Normandy or Poitou, and many knights' fees were divided into halves or thirds: clearly a tenant holding one half of a knight's fee could not repay by military service. In 1215 John wrote to Geoffrey the Marshal, justiciar of Ireland, urging him to ensure that Reginald Finegal should get free seisin of his fiefs in Ireland 'for which to us and to our heirs, he and his heirs will do the feudal service of half a knight'. How was his service to be done? Moreover, as has already been shown, many barons were no longer serving with their full quotas, so John had the problem of enforcing the full service due. Finally, many barons were objecting to service overseas as clause 7 of the Unknown Charter reveals: 'I grant to my tenants that they shall not be required to do military service outside England except in Normandy and the British Isles *et hoc decenter*.' Such were the problems of military service which John had to face.

Richard had tried to overcome one of the problems in 1194 by demanding the service of only one-third of his knights, hoping that they would serve for three times as long as forty days. This plan failed, but he was more successful in 1197 when his tenants combined to send just 300 knights for service in Normandy; this applied only to his tenants whose main lands were in England. Those tenants, on the other hand, whose lands were mainly in Normandy, could be shipped over to Normandy since their service did not start until they actually arrived there. John was less fortunate than Richard, perhaps because he was a less imposing personality. In 1201 several earls confronted him at Leicester and tried to use overseas service to blackmail privileges from him, thus implying that John had no right to insist on overseas service. As a result William Marshal and Roger de Lacy took one hundred *stipendiarii* to Normandy, financed by the rest of John's tenants who, after a meeting at Portsmouth, returned home. Similarly four years later, Wendover and Coggeshall both record that the tenants assembled and contributed towards sending just a few knights to Normandy (**46**).

Alternatively John was prepared to pay his tenants for their feudal service. Holt has suggested that the army assembled in April 1213 received prests long before the traditional forty-day limit was up: the army was summoned for 21 April and prests were issued on 22 May (**22**), while, according to the Mise Rolls, *dona* or cash gifts were paid to knights at Winchelsea on 30 April. The Irish army of

85

1210 had received prests before sailing from Pembroke and on two further occasions in Ireland itself. Prests appear to have covered both incidental expenses and bonus incentives for service; usually they were loans, though repayment was often pardoned. Prests and the development of scutage solved the problem of the divided knight's fee: the king could ask one of the knights to serve as the representative of his one or two colleagues and pay him from the scutage levied from the others. Thus in practice feudalism created problems of service, which were also solved by the use of mercenaries, one of the barons' chief grievances in 1215.

F. M. Powicke believes that the basis of John's army in Normandy, especially after 1205, was mercenary rather than feudal (**46**). Feudal aids and scutage as well as tallages and loans all served to provide mercenary troops and captains for the defence of Normandy and later its attempted recovery. Warfare in the twelfth century revolved around castles and siege techniques so that in Normandy such fortresses as Chateau Gaillard, Vaudreuil and Loches needed permanent commanders and garrisons. In 1200 Gerard of Fournival was given land to the value of £40 for his service in Normandy, and two years later Simon of Haveret canvassed support from the knights of Flanders and Brabant. Such was the value of a trusted soldier whose reliability in Normandy was sure. Many knights, moreover, were rewarded by money fiefs, since frequent enfeoffments in the twelfth century had depleted the royal demesne (**95**): instead of a fief a knight received a pension in cash as a retainer for his military service. Reginald D'Ammartin, count of Boulogne, and William, count of Holland, received money fiefs of 1000 and 400 marks during the critical times of 1213. The previous year John had offered money fiefs to several Flemish knights if they would break with Philip; several accepted, so that Philip refused to pay the money fiefs they held of him. The money fief was a useful method of gaining temporary military support, indicated by the fact that the largest number were granted during the critical years of 1200–4. Other mercenaries, knights, footsoldiers, archers, or mere men at arms fought for a fixed period at a fixed wage, ranging from 6s per day for commanders to 8d per day for men at arms. Although these wages were high the service was reliable, especially for castle garrisons and the provision of archers for campaigns in the Welsh mountains. Often, however, mercenaries caused problems: Brabançons were 'parriahs' living on plunder, to the detriment of the king's reputation. It was not unknown, either, for rival bands of mercenaries to make war against each other. Thus John was forced to extract an oath from Louvre-caire, a Norman commander, that his men would refrain from attacking the countryside; it was therefore no surprise that in 1215, the barons should insist on the expulson of such men as Fawkes des Breaute and Gerard D'Athée as part of the agreement; they were mercenaries who had come into the king's favour and been given official posts and pensions and often aroused local anger and resentment. John also kept knights in his own household called 'bachelors'; these under John of Bassingbourne were given lands or payments in expectation of future service, the only condition being their personal dependence on the king. Prestwich indeed has seen the household knight as the basis of the Norman-Angevin military system (**102**).

There was a fourth group which made up an Angevin army, the national levy. The Saxon *fyrd* had been an army composed of all freeholders summonded at the king's command; in 1181 Henry II's Assize of Arms had extended the duty to all burgesses, artisans or traders enjoying an annual revenue of at least 16 marks. Michael Powicke has shown that the military service of the people was still indispensable (**48**). The Assizes of Arms distinguished between those freemen of 16 marks income and the general levy of all men for the hue and cry and other local emergencies. The two crisis periods of John's reign precipitated further development in the national levy of freemen: in 1205 burgesses were ordered to muster under their city constables and *rustici* under the Hundred constables in an attempt to provide a home guard in case Philip attacked. The punishment for refusal was confiscation or fine, a non-feudal punishment indicating a non-feudal levy. In 1209 this was connected to the general oath of fealty made, according to the chroniclers, by all freemen. In 1211, when papal deposition was rumoured and French attack threatened, sheriffs were ordered, Wendover records, to summon 'all earls, barons and knights and all other freemen and subjects, from whom-soever they hold, provided they are capable of bearing arms and have done homage and allegiance to us. . . . And no man who can bear arms should refuse under penalty of culvertage and life-servitude'. Sheriffs indeed were ordered to bring a list of all who refused to the Dover muster of that year. The Prest Roll records the payment of those who attended, though for payment distinction was mabe between feudal forces and national levy. Powicke has emphasised that the reason for John's failure against the barons in 1215–16 was that, although he had a full complement of mercenary captains and troops, he could not summon either the feudal host or the national levy against the barons (**48**).

7 The King, the Barons and the Church

THE PROBLEM OF CHURCH AND STATE

In the middle of the twelfth century the power of the Roman Church had increased in England: in his survey of the reign of Stephen, R. H. C. Davis has written:

> In the course of the reign the Church had established a real ascendancy. At Stephen's accession it had demanded and obtained its liberty. When Stephen had violated that liberty by arresting three bishops, it had put him on trial and forced him to appeal to Rome and in 1141 at a Legatine Council it had proclaimed the Empress (Matilda) 'Lady of the English'. In the latter part of the reign the Pope had deposed one archbishop of York and established another in the teeth of royal opposition, while the Archbishop of Canterbury had attended a Papal Council in defiance of the king and refused to anoint his son Eustace. There could be no doubts that the doctrine of High Papalism had taken root in England and that the authority of the Church was greater than it had ever been (**14,** p. 127).

Stephen's successor, Henry II, however, determined to emphasise the central control of the monarchy over every facet of English life, and the Church was not to be immune. As the agent of his centralisation Henry appointed his friend and chancellor, Thomas Becket, to the see of Canterbury in 1160 and though this, as is well known, turned out to be a mistake, the personal quarrel that ensued revealed the basic ideological conflict of Church and State. In the Constitutions of Clarendon of 1164 [**doc. 2**] Henry attempted to draw the dividing line between temporal and ecclesiastical spheres of influence: clause 3 stated that

> Clerks cited and accused of any matter shall, when summoned by the king's justice, come before the king's court to answer there concerning matters which shall seem to the king's court to be

answerable there and before the ecclesiastical court for what shall seem to be answerable there, but in such a way that the justice of the king shall send to the court of Holy Church to see how the case is there tried. And if the clerk be convicted or shall confess then the Church ought no longer to protect him.

If found guilty and degraded by the Church, the clerk should be returned to the king's court for punishment according to secular law. Further, although the king attempted to define certain matters, like pleas of debt, which lay within temporal authority rather than ecclesiastical, the ultimate definition was still not clear. Henry's claims that no tenant in chief should be excommunicated without his permission (cl. 7); that churchmen who held of the King in Chief were answerable like lay tenants (cl. 11); and that vacancies were to continue as the prerogative of kings, were still only vaguely accepted. Moreover, his insistence on preventing appeals to Rome or free movement of bishops to Rome without his leave (cl. 4 and 8) would be very difficult for the Universal Church to accept. Henry also emphasised his rights in episcopal elections (cl. 12): they should be conducted in the royal chapel and homage to the king should precede consecration by the Church.

Parallel with the growth of centralised monarchy and common law in England in the twelfth century there occurred much centralisation and enlarged control of the papacy which proceeded largely through the development of canon law. The two lawyer popes, Alexander III and then Innocent III, emphasised their sovereignty over the Church Universal, the *Societas Christiana*: Innocent's famous statement that 'we hold the highest position in the Church, for others are called to a share in the responsibility, but we alone have received the plenitude of power' had obvious implications for the temporal rulers of Europe. They were brought into contact with the Papacy by the various collections of canon law decretals, particularly the famous *Decretum* of Gratian published in 1140. Mrs Mary Cheney has shown that England was in very close touch with the papacy after about 1140 (**79**). Three of the decretals of Alexander III, for instance, answer specifically English questions, and the new marriage ceremony, published by the pope in 1175, was accepted in England very soon afterwards. Alexander also held two Church councils, at Tours in 1163 and the Lateran in 1179, as a result of which appeals to Rome increased from those wanting clarification of various points of the new laws. By the 1190s a school of canon lawyers had grown up at Oxford and several English clerics became experts, such men as Gerard Purcell, bishop of Coventry in 1187 and Richard le Morins, the prior of Dunstable in 1202. Furthermore, papal centralisation was enforced by the Church hierarchy. Bishops and priests and special legates *a latere* sent from Rome to supervise and correct a local church in the name of the Pope and the canons of the Church Fathers. Hubert Walter was legate in England from 1195 to 1198 and during these years he held a provincial council at York, as well as making a legatine tour in which he proceeded, at Lichfield, 'in the order which the Roman see has prescribed for us, to uproot anything that we see to need uprooting and to implant better things' (**9**, pp. 121–2). Hubert also acted as the pope's judge delegate: usually appeals to Rome were reverted by the pope to the Province of their origin to be dealt with, on his behalf, by a local judge delegate. Hubert acted in this capacity for at least six important appeals such as that concerning the earl of Warenne and the Abbey of Cluny. Thus a picture appears of expanding papal control over English life and law, which was to come into conflict with the centralisation of the monarchy practised by Henry II and John.

John's reaction to the death of Hubert Walter in 1204 is reputed to have been the exclamation, 'Now for the first time am I King of England!' The chroniclers certainly agree that Hubert, as archbishop, had a great influence on royal policy, mitigating the cruelty of Richard according to one, restraining the tyranny of John according to another. Hubert was one of a tradition of archbishops with a love of power and no small administrative ability. In 1199 he had refused to agree to the election of Gerald the Welshman to the see of St David's, since Gerald had had designs to create a rival metropolitan see in Wales. Further, of the fifteen bishops elected in the Province of Canterbury during Hubert's time there, most were administrators of the same brand as Hubert himself (**9**). Not only did he affect a reconciliation between John and the Cistercians after a quarrel over taxation, he also played an important part in 1200 in the issue of criminous clerks. Clearly the primate of England was an important administrator as well as ecclesiastic, but equally clearly canon law could not allow the king to choose his successor at will. For this reason the election of 1205 and the interdict, the war between king and pope, were of vital importance to both parties.

THE INTERDICT

The excommunication of the king in 1209 and the rumour of papal deposition in 1212 created a dilemma for John's clerical and lay subjects. Robert FitzWalter on his arrival in France after his conspiracy in 1212 is supposed to have told Pandulf, the papal legate, that he had conspired against his king because he was excommunicated. Moreover, Wendover records that in 1213 many refused to pay scutage for an expedition to Poitou until the king was first absolved of his excommunication. In both cases the sentence was used as an excuse, but what part did the interdict play in building up opposition to the king? The problem for the barons had been enunciated in a letter from Langton at the beginning of the interdict in 1207:

> By your swords as by ours the same Church is defended. . . .
> Those among you who have authority over others, saving your
> loyalty to the king, have received their homage, and if they break
> their oath at the will or command of lesser lords, they are regarded
> as traitors and perjurors. In exactly the same way fealty is pro-
> mised to kings, saving loyalty to the superior lord, the Eternal
> King, who is King of Kings and Lord of Lords. Hence whatever
> service is rendered to the temporal king to the prejudice of the
> Eternal King is undoubtedly an act of treachery. And so, my
> beloved children, Holy Church has decreed that, if a rebel
> persists in schism, his men are absolved from the fealty which they
> owe him.

This statement, to the legally-minded men of the Middle Ages, implied the possible break up of the feudal allegiance of subject to king: it was tantamount to a legal justification of revolt. It is impossible, however, to assess what part this played in the build up of the baronial opposition: certainly Robert FitzWalter and some of the barons in 1213 used it as an excuse, certainly three Welsh princes may have been absolved of their fealty by the pope in 1212, and certainly Philip Augustus was encouraged to invade England by papal legates like Pandulf, and also to make alliances with English and Welsh princes [doc. 9]. Moreover, Professor Holt has shown that in the last two years of the interdict ecclesiastical and secular opinion grew closer together in England (24, p. 131). Langton and the conspirators of 1212 shared dissatisfaction at John's delays in putting the pope's terms into effect: not only did he destroy the castles of Robert and Eustace and delay the assessment of their damages, but he also postponed the financial settlement with the bishops. Finally John's submission to the pope and his surrender of the kingdom robbed both the barons and Philip Augustus of legal justification: neither could attack a king who was a vassal of Holy Church, though it must be admitted that the destruction of his fleet at Damme was an equally important factor in preventing Philip's intended invasion, and not even John's Crusading Vows in March 1215 could prevent the baronial *diffidatio* at the beginning of May.

The monastic annals indicate that, for most of the period of interdict, John enjoyed the support of all of the laity—they all mention the homage of 1209—and the majority of the clergy. Although many bishops fled overseas or to Scotland, this did not prevent the continuation of clerical activity, for the overall administration of the Church was little affected by the absence of the bishops. Long periods of vacancy and much absenteeism had left each diocese an administrative machine which worked without the bishop. Since there were few clerical exiles apart from the bishops, and since Church administration continued almost as usual—there was no interruption in Church courts or pleas of advowson—it seems that the clergy at least passively accepted the situation. Four new bishops, Chichester, Exeter, Lincoln and Lichfield, were elected, but not consecrated, during the period, and all were loyal to John. In addition Professor Cheney has pointed to the growth of national feeling among English clerics, especially those in Rome and especially after the loss of Normandy (**8**); the absence of episcopal visitations during the interdict would, moreover, allow the lesser clergy more freedom. All these factors indicate that John's support from clerics would not diminish during the interdict, although many, deprived by the cessation of divine service of the opportunity to exercise their priestly pre-eminence, would argue that the king was at fault.

Some would also argue that the king brought the interdict on England merely for his own financial gain. His basic policy to dissuade the clergy from their obedience to Rome was not anger and threats to slit the noses of clergy as Wendover indicates, but rather 'economic sanctions' (**75**). In 1208 royal custodians were appointed for the lands and goods of Ely and Lincoln, and presumably also for the sees of other bishops. The benefices and movable goods of the lower clergy were entrusted to the local sheriff and four men of each vill. However, this initial general confiscation lasted only a few weeks for bishops and abbots could fine with the king for the recovery of their property: the Bury Annals record that 'the king arranged to confiscate all ecclesiastical revenues and converted them for the most part to his own use. But out of reverence for St Edmund, he granted the abbey of Bury its former liberty in all respects.' The Annals of Waverley reveal a similar picture: 'The king disseised all ecclesiastical persons of all their goods and possessions, but afterwards made restitution to the religious.' Professor Cheney believes that most bishops and abbots fined for the recovery of their lands (**76**), for the record evidence, like sheriffs' returns and Chancery rolls says nothing of a regular income from Church lands to the Exchequer. In addition to these fines, the king received custodies of sees which were vacant or where the bishop had gone into exile. Canterbury, Durham and York were all vacant throughout the interdict, though John's predecessors had kept long vacancies, so this was not unusual. Moreover, as Howells has shown, John tallaged bishoprics regularly during each vacancy to increase his profits (**25**), though some of the land was granted out temporarily to supporters of the Crown like Geoffrey FitzPeter the justiciar. Ten sees are difficult to account for: the Close Roll records that the bishops of Norwich and Winchester recovered possession in April 1208, though there is no record of whether they paid for the privilege. Similarly the bishops of Bath, Salisbury and Hereford recovered possession in 1208, but later lost it. It was, however, largely exiled bishops who suffered financial loss: the Mise Roll reveals that in 1209 Ralph of Parmentarius was given £1,000 from the profits of five bishoprics, two of which were the sees of exiles, the other three being vacant. Of the monastic houses accounting on the Pipe Roll nearly all were vacant, so that John would have enjoyed their income whether there was an interdict or not. Thus John made little extra profit from the interdict beyond what was legally his because of vacancy; it is difficult to estimate a figure, though Richardson and Sales accept the amount of £100,000 recorded in the Red Book of the Exchequer (**50**, p. 355).

THE CHURCH AND THE BARONS' REVOLT

Although John's surrender to the pope had allayed all rumours of papal deposition, scotched the intended invasion of Philip Augustus, and broken the pretext which the barons had for rebellion, during the last year of the Interdict, as we have shown, there was increasing personal contact between clergy and barons. The terms demanded by Innocent on 27 February 1213 [**doc. 16**] included the restoration of Robert FitzWalter and Eustace de Vesci, for in exile with Robert was William FitzWalter, archdeacon of Hereford, and with Eustace was John the vicar of Ferriby and Elias of Dereham, Langton's steward. This clerical support for the barons was based more on personal connection than on hostility to an excommunicated king, so John's submission to Rome did little to break it. Indeed William FitzWalter, John of Ferriby and Elias of Dereham together with Simon Langton, the archbishop's brother, were the intellectual élite of the baronial party in 1215 (**24,** p. 190). Further, the baronial cause benefited from clerical wealth. The Bishop of Lincoln, Hugh of Wells, left considerable sums of money in his will in 1212 to baronial families, especially the Mandevilles, although he also left 608 marks to repay his debts to the king; in fact during his lifetime Hugh had loaned money to prominent barons like Simon of Kyme. Stephen Langton, too, loaned as much as 7000 marks to various magnates. But all these are relatively isolated examples; the majority of churchmen remained loyal to the king, especially after his submission to Rome, his charter to the Church in November 1214 and his decision to take the Cross in March 1215. Although John was tardy in his reparations to the Church, most clergy would accept the pope's lead after July 1213.

Much controversy has occurred among historians over the role and views of Langton during the years leading up to Magna Carta. Stubbs saw the archbishop as the instigator of baronial unrest in an attempt to recover the freedom of all Englishmen from the tyranny of the Angevins (**62**). Powicke in his excellent biography has outlined the archbishop's aims thus: 'the maintenance of the royal confidence, the observation of the coronation oath, the restoration of union and order and the restatement of English custom in the light of new necessities . . . Magna Carta was regarded by Langton as an elaboration of the Coronation oath' (**47,** pp. 111–12). Unfortunately both Stubbs and Powicke follow Wendover far too closely; they both accept that chronicler's account of Langton's taking the barons aside at St Paul's in John's absence in 1213 and introducing to them the Charter and Laws of Henry I. Painter similarly sees Langton as the coordinator of the reforms wanted by the barons into a

statement of law (**37,** p. 276), while Richardson and Sayles emphasise that Langton was a confirmed papalist, standing fast on papal
principles even when the pope was prepared to bargain for a compromise (**50,** pp. 342 and 356–9). The arguments of Professor Holt
seem the most compelling: Langton was a moderator and mediator
attempting to keep the peace (**24**). Wendover cannot be trusted since
there is little to corroborate his stories either in the other chroniclers,
or in the official records. When the northern barons refused the
scutage of 1213, John headed north but was intercepted at
Northampton by Langton, whose aim was the preservation of peace,
not the defence of the barons; John had just confirmed his coronation
oath in July, and Langton did not want the whole dispute to break
out again, so he urged John to proceed against the northerners by
legal and judicial methods. Moreover, when Langton met the barons
at St Paul's and, according to Wendover, presented them secretly
with Henry I's Charter, he was really more concerned with tying up
the loose ends of the Interdict. Langton did have access to Henry's
Charter, but not in the same text as the one Wendover mentions,
and his sermon at St Paul's contained no reference to his willingness
to join the barons. In fact even the neighbouring Bury Chronicle,
which is especially detailed for 1213, makes no mention of this
occurrence. During the negotiations that followed Langton was
always present, but not as one of the barons' representatives. Letters
of safe-conduct from John to the barons name him, along with
William Marshal, as a mediator; the Pope's letters of 19 March
1215, the '*Triplex Forma Pacis*', assume that he will mediate and in fact
rebuke him for his failure to prevent the quarrel between king and
barons. Finally, the 'Articles of the Barons' present him as a mediator: clauses on hostages, unjust amercements and disseisins committed by the Angevins are given support by 'the judgment of the
archbishop and those he wished to summon with him'. These
clauses all involve pledges of faith on the king's privilege as a
crusader, so Langton was acting within the principles of the Church.
He was not a baronial leader.

Moreover, Holt has depicted Innocent III as a defender of legal
principle rather than a narrow protector of the Church (**24,** p. 142).
After John's Charter to the Church and the mission of Walter
Mauclerc to Rome to ensure papal support, Innocent wrote his
three letters of 19 March. His letter to the barons condemned their
conspiracy; any future appeal to the king ought to be made with

reverence, not with arms, and if they refused to comply with these terms, Langton was empowered to excommunicate them. By a further letter of 1 April, moreover, Innocent ordered the barons to pay the Poitevin scutage. This solution was intended by Innocent as a legal decision; since 1213 he had been John's feudal overlord and was now only exercising the judicial function of overlordship. As Painter has said, 'John had gained a vigorous, determined, powerful and none too discriminating ally' (**37,** p. 199). In his letter to the pope of 29 May in which he justified his own conduct over the previous months John emphasised the legality of his position as well as his crusading vows [**doc. 16.**] It was to Innocent the lawyer that he was appealing. Even after the signing of the Charter John could count on his ally. In July he asked Innocent to annul the Charter and early in August Innocent's letter of 18 June arrived in England requesting Langton to excommunicate the barons and later his letter of 7 July condemning Langton's delay and ordering the sentence to be pronounced. It is to the events that followed the Charter that we must now turn.

Part Four

THE
GREAT CHARTER
1215

8 The Charter

THE THOUGHT BEHIND IT

Ralph of Coggeshall believed that Magna Carta [**doc. 20**] was granted to put an end to the 'evil customs which the father and brother of the king had created to the detriment of the Church and Kingdom, along with those abuses which the king himself had added'. Exactly what were the terms framed by Chancery scribes after a series of discussions in mid-June 1215? Since many of the barons were hostile to the king and the threat of civil war was a real one, the Charter was clearly intended as a peace treaty, offering privileges to the barons in return for their support. On the other hand, it may be regarded as the first statute, emphasising the supremacy of law—it certainly was different from any previous grant of privileges—or even as a new statement of political theory, a solution to the medieval problem of relating divine right monarchy to a feudal and contractual political structure. Finally, what of the barons? Can we accept, with Stubbs and Tout, that they were largely responsible for the terms of the Charter (**62, 65**); can we agree with Powicke that since many of them had held office in local or central government, they would have the legal knowledge to impose limitations on the king (**47**)? Or is it more likely that Langton and his bishops, or perhaps William Marshal, were more responsible (**35, 41**)? With the increase in lay literacy in the twelfth century, and the increasing share the barons had in administration, it is possible to see them not only defending their feudal privileges but even protecting the king's justice and the rights of the 'community of the Whole Realm'.

As was customary in the framing of Charters, the first clause was given to the Church. This was hardly a concession: John had surrendered his kingdom to papal overlordship in 1213, granted a

Charter guaranteeing free election of bishops in 1214 and taken crusading vows in March 1215. As a result most of the bishops were royalists during the civil war, nine of the sixteen being named in the Preamble of the Charter and only one, Giles de Braose, bishop of Hereford, being a known enemy of the king. Professor Cheney has suggested, indeed, that the influence of Langton and the bishops is revealed, not only in the first clause of the Charter, which was not included in the Articles of the Barons, but also in the basic principle of the Charter, that 'the king was below the law, that peace and justice were the objects of civil government' (**78,** p. 270).

After the Church, the feudal interests of the barons were protected by the next series of clauses, which must have been intended as insurance against Coggeshall's 'evil customs'. The definition of reliefs as £100 for a barony and 100s for a knight's fee (cl. 2) and the preservation of feudal custom over wardship and marriage (cl. 3–8) indicate the nature of baronial grievances; so too does the safe-guarding of baronial rights against unscrupulous scutages and aids (cl. 12, 14, 15) and the limitation of feudal military service to 'that which is owed' (cl. 16); further in clause 52 the king promised to restore his lands to anyone unlawfully disseised during his own reign and that of Richard I. In all this it is possible to see not only baronial demands for privileges, but also an appeal for customary law and just treatment according to its terms. The emphasis placed on the laws of Henry I and the coronation oath revealed an interest in good government that was not confined to Langton and the bishops.

Much controversy has centred on those clauses of the Charter dealing with royal justice and administration, typified by the vague and general clause 40: 'To no one will we sell, to no one will we deny or delay right or justice', a principle re-echoed more specifically in clauses 39 and 52. Other clauses are more detailed, dealing with writs (cl. 34, 36), the laws of the forest (cl. 44, 47, 48), law courts (cl. 17–19) and amercements (cl. 20–2). McKechnie, believing that Magna Carta was the barons' attempt to secure their feudal privileges, stated that, by cl. 34, the barons were refusing to be robbed of their feudal right to decide cases between themselves and their tenants in their baronial courts (**32**). Now this clause reads as follows: 'The writ called "Praecipe" shall not, in future, be issued to anyone, in respect of any holding whereby a freeman may lose his court.' In the twelfth century the legal treatise known as Glanville, written in the reign of Henry II, describes the writ *Praecipe* as:

When anyone complains to the king or his justices concerning his fief or his freehold, if the complaint be such as ought to be determined in the king's court, or if the king is willing that (*dominus rex vellit*) it be determined there, then the party making the complaint shall receive the following writ of summons: 'The king to Sheriff X; command (*praecipe*) N that without delay he restore to R the land of which R complains he has been dispossessed by N. If he fails to restore the land summon him to attend my court or that of my justices on the day appointed' (**15,** p. 463).

Miss Hurnard has recently criticised McKechnie's view that clause 34 was a statement of baronial feudal privilege (**90**). She has shown that baronial courts did not have exclusive rights to cases concerning land, even in the reign of Henry I; then cases between men holding land of different feudal lords were tried in the county court, and cases between barons were tried in the king's court. The expression *Dominus rex vellit* should be translated 'If the king is willing' not 'If the king decides'; there is no question of royal tyranny about the writ *praecipe*, it did not attempt to remove to the king's court cases which ought to be tried in baronial courts. Miss Hurnard has thus squashed the view that by clause 34 the barons were trying to recover feudal rights seized by the Angevin tyrants.

Powicke, moreover, has shown that the beneficial effects of clause 39 were not confined to the barons (**100**). The term *nulli liberi homines*, no free men, was used in six clauses of Magna Carta, and Powicke has stressed that churchmen, citizens and statesmen were present at the June discussions as well as the barons; these drafters would not overlook the increasing significance of the freeman in English legal and economic life, since all men needed protection against arbitrary arrests. Moreover, judgment by peers and/or the law of the land was an attempt to return to judicial procedures in use before the reforms of Henry II. The term *lex terrae* was rather used as inclusive of all legal forms introduced by Henry including indictments, writs and possessory assizes. It could also be equated with baronial legal combat or juries of presentment and recognition, depending on the case concerned. Like clause 52, clause 39 was an appeal for good justice according to the accepted formulae introduced by the Angevins; and this was to be justice for all free men, not only barons: who were the beneficiaries of clause 40? ('To no one will we sell . . .') Who were the beneficiaries of clause 36 which insisted that the writ *de odio et atia* be granted freely, not sold? Clearly all the judicial clauses of the Charter were of wider benefit, available to more than just the baronial class.

There is even the beginning of the concept of the rights of the whole realm in Magna Carta, a concept which was to reveal itself much more clearly in the representative assemblies of the thirteenth century. The Dunstable Annalist described the Charter as one that 'concerned the liberties of the kingdom of England': clause 48 of the Articles referred to 'all those customs and liberties which the king has granted to the kingdom'. Even the very lowest social ranks were beneficiaries of clause 45 by which no one ignorant of the law could assume a legal office such as sheriff, bailiff or constable. Finally, the barons devoted the last three clauses to security, to try to prevent John's rescinding of the Charter once his position of strength was recovered. They had to do something for the bishops refused to undertake that the king would not revoke the Charter by appeal to the pope. So the security clause, 61, was needed: 'We have granted all the aforesaid things for God, for the reform of our Realm, and for the better settling of the quarrel which has arisen between us and our barons.' If John broke the terms of the Charter, 'the 25 barons with the commune of the whole realm (*Communa totius terre*) shall distrain and distress us in every way they can'. It has been suggested that this political *Communa* was nothing more than the feudal community, the king's tenants in chief; yet this is unlikely for the king's court of Common Pleas was *Communa Placita*, and Gervase of Canterbury referred to the *Communia* as the County constabulary organisation for local military levies; finally Henry II's Juries of Presentment were thought to represent the *communia*. In clause 61 of Magna Carta the 25 represented the baronial ranks; the *communa totius terre* referred to the whole body of freemen of the country. Thus these security clauses, along with the restoration of all hostages (cl. 49), the removal of the king's mercenaries (cl. 50–1) and the compensation to Welsh and Scots (cl. 56–9), emphasise the peace treaty nature of this Charter.

Was this, then, a peace treaty with which the king could be satisfied? How much, in fact, did he surrender? In the twelfth century John of Salisbury in his 'Policraticus' pointed out that the word *rex* was derived from *recte*: the king should give his people good law and automatically follow it himself. But he was king by divine right; he was never responsible to his subjects, only for them, to

God. Moreover, royal charters bear the title 'Johannes, Dei gratia, rex Anglorum . . .' Now in England kingship was intimately connected with the royal demesne which was inherited by the principles of family and land law: hence the English kings, unlike Holy Roman Emperors, were hereditary rulers, they could not be elected. As the Saxon functions of kingship were expanded during the twelfth century, all law and justice became the king's, all writs published by his Chancery were his own voice. Even in 1234 Bracton could write that 'our lord the king cannot be summoned or receive a command from anyone', which means, of course, that he was a sovereign ruler. It seems then that English monarchy was badly treated by Magna Carta: not only was the king deprived of his divine right powers to be obeyed even when ruling badly, but also he lost full control over law and justice. Of course in theory all justice remained the king's, but clause 61 would distrain him if his justice were not reasonable and good. The king was now under the law in the constitutional sense. Small wonder that the Charter did not end the civil war.

THE MORROW OF THE CHARTER

The problem of Magna Carta was putting it into effect. Ideally the Charters were to be read out in the county courts and other gatherings of local officials; but Charters were not sent to sheriffs, rather were they distributed gradually by Elias of Dereham and Henry de Vere between mid-June and mid-July. Even as late as 22 July Elias was given six copies to be issued to county courts: consequently there must have been some delay and uncertainty about the means of enforcing them. Further, as Professor Holt has written, 'The Charter must have started many a local war' (**24,** p. 250): since the terms and phraseology were so vague, disputes over interpretation followed and needed a definitive statement in solution. Such clauses as number 2, 'And anyone who owes less shall give less according to the ancient usage of fiefs'; number 4, 'The guardian of the land of an heir . . . shall not take from the land more than the reasonable revenues, customary dues and services'; and number 52, ordering the restoration of anyone 'unjustly' disseised, all needed further definition. Moreover, although the security clause enforced distraint on an unjust king, it contained no further provisions for dealing with him if he continued to object to the barons' constraint. The problem of Magna Carta was one of interpretation: the baronial view of clause 52 deprived the king of his royal right of patronage; the baronial view of clause 61 deprived him of his sovereign power. He could not accept their interpretation.

On 19 June, the day that peace was made, John certainly tried to enforce some of the terms of the Charter. Peter des Roches was replaced as justiciar by Hubert de Burgh; and several barons recovered lost territory: Ruald FitzAlan, for example, regained Richmond castle, and Earl David of Huntingdon recovered Fotheringay castle. The Close Roll reveals the restoration of hostages to John de Lacy and others, and estates to Eustace de Vesci, Gilbert de Gant, Roger de Montbegon and Robert de Brus, all members of the Twenty-Five. On the other hand the king was not enthusiastic about certain other restorations: Nicholas de Stuteville who lost Knaresborough in 1205 could only recover it if he had been deprived by the law of the land. John did not restore his lands but the baronial committee of Twenty-Five decided that he ought to hold them. Similarly the claim of Geoffrey de Mandeville to hold the strategically placed Tower of London was postponed and the Tower temporarily placed in the hands of Stephen Langton. Moreover, John was in no hurry to dismiss his mercenary leaders: he did order Hugh de Boves to dismiss several of those in Dover on 23 June, but on 2 July he reinforced his own bodyguard with the mercenaries of Geoffrey de Martigny, a Poitevin leader, and on 13 August he was arranging for the payment of Poitevin mercenaries coming over to England from the Continent. Mercenary leaders, in fact, never left England: Philip Mark remained in Nottingham throughout the civil war, and Fawkes des Breauté and Savary de Mauléon never left the kingdom.

To complicate the uncertainty of the period, there is in the Public Records Office a treaty between John and Robert FitzWalter, largely concerning the custody of London, which most authorities date about 19 June (**24, 81**), though Richardson sees it as part of the Oxford Council of 16 July (**104**). The treaty laid down that the barons were to hold London until 15 August, oaths of obedience were to be taken to the Twenty-Five and both sides were to continue to hold their own castles. Moreover, if the king in any way neglected to fulfil the terms of the Charter, the barons were to continue to hold London (**81**). By such political bargaining the barons were blackmailing the king to accept and enforce Magna Carta. Possession of London was crucial to the rebels throughout 1215: at the beginning of July Robert FitzWalter wrote to William de Albini of Belvoir that the tournament, arranged for 6 July at Stamford would now have to be held near Staines, because of the need to secure possession of the capital (**24**, p. 250). Moreover, a second document, the Lambeth Memorandum, reveals the number of knights bound to serve each member of the Twenty-Five if the king failed to enforce the Charter (**73**). It seems unlikely now, that the former picture of peace during the weeks following the Charter can be substantiated. Clearly Magna Carta was by no means a final peace, even to contemporaries.

To settle the disputes the two sides raranged to meet on 16 July at Oxford. Certainly the barons of the southern half of England attended, though it seems possible that some northerners had formed a separate rebel group and, according to Walter of Coventry, recommenced hostilities in the north. The meeting at Oxford did, however, settle some problems: Hubert de Burgh was given Norfolk and Suffolk, Robert de Vaux Cumberland, though he failed to take possession of Carlisle, and other restorations were effected by letters patent of 24 July. Basically, however, the meeting failed. The barons still refused to acknowledge their obligations to the Crown in writing, for clearly such obligations were incompatible with their interpretation of the security clause of the Charter. Moreover, the barons were unwilling to surrender London and the king would still not acknowledge Geoffrey de Mandeville's claim to the Tower. A month later, on 20 August, the barons again assembled at Oxford; this time John refused to attend but sent messengers to say that he had kept his part of the bargain according to the treaty with Robert FitzWalter, now it was up to the barons to fulfil their side and restore London. Civil war was the direct result of the failure of these negotiations.

Meanwhile the pope had been emphasising to both parties the legal principles at stake and pressing the barons to accept John as their rightful king. Innocent may well have seen in the security clause the growth of a rival power to his own overlordship in England. But he seems, as a canon lawyer, to have been more genuinely interested in the legal principle. On 7 July he issued a mandate to Pandulf, his legate, the bishop of Winchester and the abbot of Reading that they should command Langton to excommunicate all who disturbed the peace of the realm and place their lands under interdict. The three commissioners were also empowered to suspend Langton or any bishops who refused to accept or enforce such an excommunication. Furthermore, at some time near the end of July, probably from Oxford, John wrote to Innocent asking him to annul Magna Carta and release him from his oath to accept it. Innocent's mandate of 7 July was received about the middle of August, by which time it was completely out of date and the king appears to have made little use of it; the fact that it was sent to three commissioners rather than to Langton was, however, important. Langton had been working for peace and a settlement; now the pope had clearly taken the side of the king and chances of a compromise were ruined. Langton, of course, refused to excommunicate the rebels and was suspended, a sentence confirmed by the pope in November. The letters from the commissioners to Langton on 5 September clearly reveal the papal position: the barons were rebels from the time of their *diffidatio* in May onwards, and Magna Carta was opposed to the law of the land and the peace of the realm. Within two weeks of this letter John was confiscating the lands of his opponents and war was breaking out: the king was standing firm in the Papal decision and attempting to confirm what the commissioners had written. Meanwhile in Rome Innocent had promulgated his bull '*Et Si Carissimus*' on 24 August; annulling the Charter and requesting the barons to accept the king's grace. In an accompanying letter he urged the barons to accept papal mediation. The bull and the letter reached England probably at the end of September, but had no effect. By then civil war had begun again.

In resources for the war the king had an advantage: in his mercenary troops he had armed skilful fighting men, paid from his sources of jewels or the proceeds of the Cornish tin mines, and well horsed. He possessed, moreover, according to Painter, 149 castles as opposed to sixty held by the barons, and the sixty baronial castles were largely country houses rather than castles (**37,** p. 252). Finally, John, as the crowned king of England, was much more likely to inspire loyalty during civil war than the Twenty-Five whom contemporaries would regard as rebels, especially after the papal denunciation of '*Et Si Carissimus*'. The one real baronial strength was London, and on this they survived until the arrival of Prince Louis in 1216. (For details of the civil war, see **37,** chapter 9.) Eventually the weakness of the baronial position became more and more evident: they were rebels against their king, excommunicated by the pope and with little military power in England. Gradually they began to make their peace with the king: the count of Aumale made his peace with John in September 1215, John de Lacy in January 1216. By May of that year several barons, including Eustace de Vesci, were trying to make favourable settlements. Moreover, the bull '*Et Si Carissimus*' absolved all barons of their oaths to the Twenty-Five; thus royalists like William Marshal could feel no compunction in serving John against the remaining rebels. When Prince Louis invaded in 1216 he was received with enthusiasm by many of the Twenty-Five, but Hubert de Burgh, a man acceptable to the barons at the Council of Oxford, held Dover castle against his siege, and after John's death in October 1216, Louis's claim to the throne had little support, since opposition to John had been so largely personal.

Now, William Marshal, Ranulf of Chester and William of Salisbury not only defended the realm for the young King Henry against the foreign invader, but were also instrumental in the reissues of Magna Carta. Holt has suggested that with John dead they could at last reveal their true feelings (**24,** p. 269): several clauses of the 1215 charter were dropped and their purpose in dropping them appears to have been to uphold the strength of Angevin monarchy, while preserving the feudal statements of reasonable and just government. Perhaps the most significant omission from the reissues was the security clause: the king was to be restored to his former sovereign state. Perhaps the most striking illustration of the new peace was that although nine of the Twenty-Five were dead in 1225, nine of the remaining sixteen were witnesses of the reissue of the Charter, along with royalist barons like Marshal and Hubert de Burgh and William of Salisbury.

THE MYTH OF MAGNA CARTA

As has been shown above, Magna Carta was the product of a particular political situation; it must be judged ultimately on its meaning and significance for the men of 1215. 'It was not an exact statement of law . . . but a political document produced in a crisis' (**24,** pp. 5–6). Yet, although John may not have intended to keep its terms longer than was politically convenient, it survived the minority of his son and the political uncertainty of the later Middle Ages to be regarded by the seventeenth and eighteenth centuries as fundamental law. It is not difficult to account for this survival, for the Charter was above all vague in its phrasing: who is a 'free man' according to clause 39? What exactly is meant by the 'lawful judgment of peers' in clause 39? Above all who should define what is 'just' or 'reasonable'? Such vagueness resulted in the continual need for reinterpretation of various clauses of the Charter to suit differing social and legal conditions. Moreover, since the Charter was so imprecise lawyers could adapt, or 'distort' its terms to their own advantage. Oliver St John, in his protest against benevolences in 1615, quoted precedent, 'The law is in the statute called Magna Carta . . . that no free man be any way destroyed, but by the laws of the land.' At the ensuing trial, Bacon, for the Crown, emphasised that it was these very laws of the land that King James was protecting: 'Is it so that King James shall be said to be a violator of the liberties, laws, and customs of this kingdom?' (**64,** p. 281). The Charter too embodied for later thinkers a basic problem of political theory, the struggle between authority and the individual and the place of the law in that struggle. It did indicate that the king, authority, was subject to laws which would protect the rights of his subjects. Thus Magna Carta formed an important element in all legal and political thinking until the nineteenth century.

Its immediate success in the thirteenth century had other causes. It was helped, of course, by the continuation of the main characters of 1215 in local politics and the reading of each reissue of the Charter in every county court: in Essex in 1238, Richard de Muntfichet, one of the Twenty-Five, would undoubtedly take advantage of this opportunity to read the Forest Charter in the Shire Court (**24**). In addition, as Henry III approached maturity these same barons became afraid of a possible revival of Angevin monarchy: in 1224 they demanded confirmation of Magna Carta, and when in 1237 Henry issued a 'Small Charter' confirming all the demands of 1215 and the Charter of the Forest, the witness list included Peter des Roches, Hubert de Burgh and William de Warenne, John's advisers at Runnymede, and John de Lacy and Richard de Percy, members of the Twenty-Five. During his minority, too, Henry needed taxation and received a fifteenth for the reissue in 1225 and a thirtieth for the 'Small Charter' of 1237: redress of grievances was now being given for supply of cash (**63**). Finally, the Church too supported the reissues, for any who violated the terms of the Charters would be excommunicated.

But all this does not explain the growth in the thirteenth century of the 'myth' of Magna Carta. Miss Thompson has followed McKechnie in emphasising that the essential point about 1215 was that an anointed king had admitted that he was no longer absolute (**63, 96**). Moreover, the king was to be under the law, his prerogative limited and his powers confined, through the security clause, by the 'Community of the Realm'; and even though the security clause was omitted from the reissues, partly because the king was still a minor, the idea of the king's being controlled by written law remained. Professor Holt, too, agrees that by 1225 the Charter had become, not just a programme of the baronial party, but a statement of law (**24**), and it was to settle court cases where its vague wording needed interpretation that Magna Carta assumed its monumental importance to the thirteenth century. Even as late as 1292 and 1302 two cases appeared before Edward I where a lord claimed his court by the writ *praecipe* under clause 34 of the Charter, and there were many appeals in accordance with clause 17 which demanded the permanent establishment of the Bench at Westminster, when Henry III tried to evade the Charter by bringing a case to his court *coram rege*. Other judicial and legal clauses of the Charter were similarly evoked for support or interpreted for clarity during the thirteenth century (**63,** pp. 44–51) and there was no shortage of appeals to the feudal causes either. In York in 1290 the court recognised the rights of a widow, as in clause 7 of the Charter, to 'stay in her husband's house forty days after his death, within which period her dower shall be assigned to her'. Moreover, in 1284 Archbishop Peckham wrote to the chancellor, Robert Burnell: 'We are exceedingly astonished that you have permitted letters to go out from your chancery to disseise us, contrary to Magna Carta, of the custody of our priory at Dover.' Here reference was to clause 46. Thus Magna Carta was kept alive in the courts; it was also discussed on occasions by bodies set up for the purpose, as in 1226 when Henry III invited four knights each from eight counties to settle problems and quarrels arising over the Charter. Moreover, as McKechnie noted, various clauses of the Charter had to be reinterpreted to fit in with new problems and customs; clause 39, for instance, insisted on trial by peers, so that under Edward I a knight insisted on trial by jury of fellow-knights. Similar amendments had to be made to clauses 33 and 40. Not only is this evidence of the 'lasting practical value of Magna Carta'; it is also an indication of the continuing reference to its principle of authority confined by written law. This was why the Charter, especially the statute version of 1225 (though contemporaries did confuse the 1215 and 1225 versions) became a legend in thirteenth-century England.

In the thirteenth century, too, added justification for the Charter was provided by the 'Community of the Realm'. Henry III's use of foreign councillors like Peter des Roches and Peter des Rivaux, and his removal of the offices of justiciar, chancellor and treasurer aroused opposition which claimed to be acting on behalf of the whole realm. Between 1258 and 1267 the barons attempted to control the king's ministers: the Provisions of Oxford established a Privy Council of fifteen men nominated by the barons; it was to this Privy Council that all the king's ministers were to be responsible. In addition local government was reformed, to enable four knights of every shire to sit regularly at the county court. The Provisions were enhanced by the Statute of Marlborough of 1267 which proclaimed the rule of law and the observation of the Magna Carta: writs were to be issued against all who infringed the sacred text of 1225, thus insisting on the literal nature of the document as well as its principle. In August 1297 it was the confirmation of the Charters, Magna Carta and the Forest Charter, which enabled the Regency government of Edward II to satisfy the demands of barons and bishops and temporarily end the 'consitutional opposition' to Edward I.

Thereafter, it was on the vague but crucial clauses 39 and 40 that attention was focused. Holt has shown how Edward III's parliaments distorted clause 39: 'lawful judgment of peers' came to include trial by jury, and 'the law of the land' became 'due process of law' which entailed the use of original writs or indicting juries; finally 'no free man' became 'no man of whatever estate or condition he may be' (**24**). These were interpretations which were never intended, or even considered, in 1215, but they were fundamental in the development of Common Law. Coke wrote in the seventeenth century that 'the Great Charter and the Charter of the Forest are to be holden for the Common Law, that is, the law common to all; and that both the Charters are in amendment of the realm, that is to amend great mischiefs and inconveniences which oppressed the whole realm before the making of them'. This gave the Charters great validity, for common law was not just enacted, it was customary procedure, it was the *consuetudo regni*. Further, what to Coke was common law was soon assumed to be fundamental law: Coke condemned Stuart monopolies as 'against this great charter, because they are against the liberty and freedom of the subject, and against the law of the land' (**24,** p. 10). Thus the myth grew up. The Leveller Lilburne was arrested by the Commons in 1645 for slandering the Speaker of the House; in his defence he declared that the Commons had violated his rights guaranteed in Magna Carta, and that they 'are not to act according to their own wills and pleasure, but according to the fundamental customs and constitutions of the land'.

Not all was adulation: the Digger Winstanley, more radical than Lilburne, could condemn the Charter as a manacle 'tying one sort people to be slaves to another; clergy and gentry have got their freedom, but the common people still are slaves to work for them'. Basically, though, the history of the Charter is one of petitions for confirmation and reinterpretation; even the American colonists turned to it, along with the Bill of Rights and the Habeas Corpus Act, in establishing their independence and freedom. The growth of this myth is one of the reasons therefore why Magna Carta, and the reign of King John, are important points in English history.

Part Five

DOCUMENTS

The Coronation Charter of Henry I, 1100

Henry, king of the English, to Samson the Bishop, and Urse of Abbetot, and to all his barons and faithful vassals, both French and English, in Worcestershire, greeting.

1. Know that by the Mercy of God and by the common counsel of the barons of the whole kingdom of England I have been crowned king of this realm. And because the kingdom has been oppressed by unjust exactions, I now, being moved by reverence towards God and by the love I bear you all, make free the Church of God; so that I will neither sell nor lease its property; nor on the death of an Archbishop, or a biship, or an abbot will I take anything from the demesne of the Church or from its vassals during the period which elapses before a successor is installed. I abolish all the evil customs by which the kingdom of England has been unjustly oppressed. Some of these evil customs are here set forth.

2. If any of my barons or of my earls or of any other of my tenants shall die, his heir shall not redeem his land as he was wont to do in the time of my brother, but he shall henceforth redeem it by means of a just and lawful relief. Similarly the men of my barons shall redeem their lands from their lord by means of a just and lawful relief.

3. If any of my barons, or of my tenants, shall wish to give in marriage his daughter or his sister or his niece or his cousin, he shall consult me about the matter; but I will neither seek payment for my consent, nor will I refuse my permission, unless he wishes to give her in marriage to one of my enemies. And if, on the death of one of my barons or one of my tenants, a daughter should be his heir, I will dispose of her in marriage and of her lands according to the counsel given me by my barons. And if the wife of one of my tenants survives her husband and is without children, she shall have her dower and her marriage portion and I will not give her in marriage unless she herself consents. . . .

6. I forgive all pleas and all debts which were owing to my brother except my own proper dues, and except those things which were agreed to belong to the inheritance of others, or to concern the property which justly belonged to others. . . .

9. I remit all murder fines which were incurred before the day on which I was crowned king; and such murder fines as shall now be incurred shall be paid justly according to the law of King Edward.

10. By the common counsel of my barons I have retained the forest in my own hands as my father did before me.

11. The knights, who in return for their estate perform military service equipped with a hauberk of mail, shall hold their demesne lands quit of all gelds and all work. I make this concession as my own free gift in order that, being thus relieved of so great a burden, they may furnish themselves so well with horses and arms that they may be properly equipped and prepared to discharge my service and defend my kingdom.

12. I establish a firm peace in all my kingdom and I order that henceforth this peace shall be kept.

13. I restore to you the laws of King Edward together with such emendations as my father made with the counsel of his barons . . .

Witness: Maurice, Bishop of London . . .

At London, when I was crowned.

In Latin in *Stubbs, 'Select Charters'* (**13**), pp. 117–19; translation in *English Historical Documents* (**15**), ii, pp. 400–2.

document 2

The Constitutions of Clarendon 1164

Now of the acknowledged customs and privileges of the realm a certain part is contained in the present document, of which part these are the heads:

1. If a dispute shall arise between laymen, or between clerks and laymen, or between clerks, concerning advowsons and presentation to churches, let it be treated and concluded in the court of the lord King. . . .

3. Clerks cited and accused of any matter shall, when summoned by the king's justice, come before the king's court to answer there concerning matters which shall seem to the king's

court to be answerable there, and before the ecclesiastical court for what shall seem to be answerable there, but in such a way that the justice of the king shall send to the court of Holy Church to see how the case is there tried. And if the clerk be convicted or shall confess, the Church ought no longer to protect him.

4. It is not lawful for archbishops, bishops and beneficed clergy of the realm to depart from the kingdom without the lord king's leave. And if they do so depart, they shall, if the king so please, give security that neither in going, nor in tarrying, nor in returning will they contrive evil or injury against the king or the kingdom. . . .

7. No one who holds of the king in chief nor any of the officers of his demesne shall be excommunicated, nor the lands of any one of them placed under Interdict, unless application shall first be made to the lord king. . . .

8. With regard to appeals if they should arise, they should proceed from the archdeacon to the bishop and from the bishop to the archbishop. And if the archbishop should fail to do justice, the case must finally be brought to the lord king, in order that by his command the dispute may be determined in the archbishop's court, in such wise that it may proceed no further without the assent of the lord king. . . .

11. Archbishop, bishops and all beneficed clergy of the realm, who hold of the king in chief, have their possessions from the lord king by barony and are answerable for them to the king's justices and officers. . . .

15. Pleas of debt under pledges of faith, or even without pledge of faith, are to lie in the justice of the king. . . .

In Latin (**13**), pp. 163–7; translation (**15**), pp. 718–22.

document 3
Wendover's account of the Canterbury election 1205

Now that the see was vacant, a group of younger monks from the Chapter immediately elected their sub prior Reginald, without the king's consent, and in the middle of the night after the election and the singing of the 'Te Deum' they raised him above the High Altar and placed him in the Archbishop's Chair. They were afraid, too, that if the king heard of the election he would try to stop it, so the sub prior went immediately to Rome on that very same night, taking with him certain monks of the Chapter and promising not to reveal his mission to anyone. This was done so that the election should be kept from the king until the monks could get the approval of the Roman Court, but the said Reginald broke his promise as soon as he reached Flanders and told all and sundry that he had been elected and that he was going to the Curia for confirmation. Moreover, he freely showed the letters he had from the convent, believing that these would promote the merits of his case. At length he reached the Curia and showed the letters to the Lord Pope and his Cardinals, and asked the papal blessing on his election; the Pope, however, decided to wait for more evidence before he made a decision.

Meanwhile the Canterbury Chapter heard that Reginald had broken his promise in Flanders, and immediately sent representatives to the king asking for the king's licence for them to choose a suitable pastor; the king kindly granted their request and pointed out to them the bishop of Norwich, a man very close to the king and one who had a greater share in the royal business than any other prelate in England. The king told the monks, further, that it would be to the advantage of both himself and the whole realm if this bishop of Norwich could be transferred to the See of Canterbury. He also asked them if he could send one of his clerks to the Chapter to put this view to them and promised great privileges for the Chapter if they would agree to it . . . and eventually in the king's presence and before a great crowd in the metropolitan church all of whom agreed with the election, John de Gray, bishop of Norwich, was shown to all the people, carried by the monks to the High Altar and placed on the Archbishop's Chair.

Wendover, *Flores Historiarum* (see p. 140), pp. 183–5.

Gervase of Canterbury's account of the Canterbury election 1205

In the year of our Lord 1205 the venerable Archbishop of Canterbury passed away and to prevent the Metropolitan Church remaining empty without a pastor for too long the monks of the Chapter diligently debated the election of a new Archbishop, as was their right. At length they celebrated the election of Reginald, their sub prior, a religious and scholarly man. When the king heard of the matter, he was furious, both because it had been done without his knowledge and agreement and because he preferred one of his own household for such a high office; and once he had intervened the bishops of the province of Canterbury, who together with certain monks of the Chapter had obtained the royal favour, disagreed with the election of Reginald. In fact they quashed it completely and changed their vote to John, bishop of Norwich, one of the king's familiars, and elected him. Thus a schism arose in the realm. . . .

The sub prior, the first elected, went immediately to Rome expecting to receive confirmation from Pope Innocent III since his election was strengthened by letters which he had from the Cathedral Chapter. He was followed by the representatives of the second party, among whom were twelve monks of Canterbury, hostile to Reginald and supporting John de Gray, and carrying letters from the Chapter, the Provincial Bishops, and the King and also hoping to secure support by bribery. . . .

The Lord Pope, however, approved neither election and in fact rejected both candidates.

In full in *'Fragmentary Chronicle' of Gervase of Canterbury*, ed. W. Stubbs, Rolls Series, 1880.

Philip Augustus's proposals to Ralph of Exoudun, count of Eu (before Easter 1206)

This is the message brought by the Earl of Augi: The king has sent me to you because he knows that you are one of the most powerful barons of Poitou and that there is no one more suitable to conduct his business in South West France. He requests you therefore to make the following agreement with him: the king surrenders to you all the land which he holds in Poitou from Easter next for five years; in addition, for making war, he will give you every year £4,000 Parisienne, and also for three months each year, one hundred knights and 1,000 foot soldiers. In return you must surrender to him your land and fortifications in Normandy for security that you will serve him faithfully, and you must command your vassals also to serve him faithfully throughout the five years. .... If you should die within the said term, moreover, the king will return your land to your wife and children according to the customary laws of Normandy. If you are willing to negotiate this agreement, the king agrees to make it with no conditions attached; if, however, you are unwilling, a similar proposal will be made to someone else. But before that he wishes to speak to you, for the land of Poitou is far distant from his Majesty and he cannot journey to it with any convenient speed.

In Latin in French Archives, *Recueil*, vol. ii.

document 6
Wendover's account of William de Braose, 1208

Among these and other similar acts of impiety King John was very much afraid that the Lord Pope would impose a punishment upon him even more serious than the Interdict, possibly by excommunicating him by name or absolving the barons of England of their fealty. Therefore, so he wouldn't lose control of his kingdom, he sent a group of soldiers to all the powerful men in the kingdom and especially to those whom he suspected of treachery, to demand hostages from them; thus if any of them in due time broke away from their loyalty, he would have the means to recall them to their homage. Many agreed to his demands, some handing over their sons, others their nephews and others their illegitimate offspring. However, when the soldiers came to William de Braose, a very important baron, and demanded hostages as they had done from the others, William's wife Matilda snatched at them and replied, 'I shall not give away my sons to your lord king John because of his shameful murder of his nephew Arthur whom he ought to have kept in honourable custody.' When her husband heard her words, he immediately hushed her and said, 'You have spoken like a foolish woman against our lord the king; for if I have offended him in any way I am prepared—and I beg my king to allow me—to make satisfaction, without hostages, according to the justice of his court and of my peers, the barons, on any day and in any place he may choose.' When the messengers had returned to the king and told him what they had heard, the king became agitated and sent his soldiers secretly to arrest William with his whole family and bring them in haste to his court. William, however, was warned by some friends and fled with his wife and family to Ireland.

Wendover, *Flores Historiarum* (see p. 140), pp. 224–5.

document 7
King John's account of William de Braose 1212

John, by the grace of God, King of England, Lord of Ireland, Duke of Normandy and Aquitaine and Count of Anjou, to all who may see this letter.

So that it may be well known to you all on what account William de Braose fled from our lands, know that the same William owed us in 1204 5,000 marks for our lands in Meath in Ireland which we gave him and that he paid only five hundred of that back. . . . And besides he owed us for the farm of Limerick for the previous five years, and from all this debt he repaid only one hundred pounds. . . . And after a further five years he was distrained, according to the custom of the realm and the law of the Exchequer, to repay his debts; but he hid his chattels in England so that they could not be found and therefore we asked our bailiff in South Wales, Gerard D'Athée, to distrain his Welsh chattels to repay his debts.

Then Matilda, William's wife, and William, Earl of Ferrar,

his nephew, and Adam de Porter, his brother in law, and other friends came to us at Gloucester and asked whether William might come to us and make satisfaction for his debts, and we agreed. He came to us at Hereford and handed over his three Welsh castles to us to be held as security for the payment of his debts. . . . And he also gave hostages, the two sons of William de Braose junior and the son of Reginald de Braose and four sons of his vassals. But he took no more care to observe this agreement than he had to keep previous ones.

After a short time when Gerard D'Athée, to whom we had granted the three castles, had requested their constables to come to receive their pay, which they did each month, William, realising that the constables were absent, attacked the three castles with his sons and a crowd of his family and supporters and all three were besieged on the same day. . . . When Gerard heard of these events he sent . . . help to those areas as best he could and William was forced to flee from place to place and eventually fled to Ireland with his wife and sons and their families.

In full in Latin in Rymer, *Foedera* (see p. 141), pp. 52–3.

document 8

Wendover reports the king's deposition 1212

At this time Stephen, Archbishop of Canterbury, and William and Eustace, the bishops of London and Ely, arrived in Rome and informed the Pope of the enormities which John had perpetrated during the Interdict in England right up to that very moment, aggravating God and His Holy Church with his savagery and cruelty. Therefore, they humbly begged the Lord Pope to help the English Church in its extremity and relieve its misery. Then the Lord Pope, after consultation with his Cardinals, Bishops and Wise Men, decided that King John should be deposed from his throne because of the desolation of his realm, and that another more worthy should succeed with Papal approval. To execute this sentence the Lord Pope wrote to the most powerful Philip, King of France, encouraging him to this good work for the remission of all his sins and so that, after John's expulsion, he and his heirs should possess the Crown of England for ever. The Pope also wrote to the barons, knights and mercenaries that they should undertake a crusade against the King of England under the leadership of the King of France. . . .

In full in Wendover, *Flores Historiarum* (see p. 140), pp. 241–2.

document 9

Letter of Llywelyn the Great to Philip Augustus, *c*.1212

To his most gracious lord, Philip, by the grace of God illustrious king of the French, greeting from Llywelyn, prince of North Wales, your faithful vassal. What can I give your lordship in return for the singular honour and priceless gift which you, the King of France, the prince of the whole world, have shown to me, your faithful vassal, by sending me your letters, under your gold seal, as witness of a treaty between the king of France and the prince of North Wales? I shall keep these letters in my strong box in a church, like sacred relics, as a perpetual testimony and memorial that I and my heirs will always be allies to you and your heirs, friends to your friends and hostile to your enemies. I hope this treaty will be inviolably observed by your royal dignity in every way; and so that I will keep it too, by the common counsel of the princes of Wales, all of whom are grouped in friendship with you in this treaty, by the witness of my seal, I promise in perpetuity to remain your vassal. And I intend to fulfil my promise. . . . I will make no treaty or peace of any kind with the English, but I and all the princes of Wales promise in unity to resist our common enemy with God's aid and to recover forcibly the castles which they have tyrannically captured and by treachery occupied. . . .

In Latin in French Archives, *Layettes du Tresor Des Chartres*, 1032.

The interdict according to the Annals of Dunstable under 1207

In the same year on Passion Sunday an Interdict was placed on the whole of England and Wales so that all relations with the Church were brought to an end, excepting those of the White Monks: and even these, after much debate, were compelled to be subject to the Interdict. The bodies of the dead were laid in unconsecrated ground without the presence of the priest; vows and purifications were made at the doors of churches . . . and on Sundays sermons were preached to the people and holy bread and water given to them outside the church while priests baptised infants inside the church. And lest some chrism be lacking for baptism, oil was used by special papal licence, and those laymen wishing to offer themselves as godparents were granted permission to come to the altar.

In the same year at Easter, the king ordered all the goods of clerks or monastic houses to be taken into his own hands, and declared that all clerks who obeyed the Pope's Interdict should leave their lands. However, after four days, when his temper cooled, lands were placed in the custody of constables. . . .

In the same year ships fled like exiles from the Cinque Ports. . . . The following went into exile: Geoffrey, archbishop of York, William of London, Eustace of Ely, Mauger of Worcester and Giles of Hereford. The bishops of Salisbury and Rochester delayed in Scotland with the king's permission, and only Winchester remained in England.

Honorius Archdeacon of Richmond was deprived of all his goods and imprisoned at Gloucester.

Anno MCCX. The king has demanded an aid from the monasteries of England, so that we at Dunstable, among others, owe him 20m. At the same time the king has declared that no pleas be conducted in England by Papal authority, with corporal punishment for any who transgress. In addition he has compelled the White Monks, through confiscation of their lands and goods, to pay a fine to him.

In full in *Annales Monastici* (see p. 140) iii, pp. 30–40.

Account of John's meeting with papal legates 1211 by Burton Annals

The Papal legates met John at Northampton at an assembly of all the earls and barons of England and addressed the Lord King as follows: 'Lord, we have travelled far to seek the peace of Holy Church and we ask your terms.' When the king replied that he did not know what they wanted, they said, 'Nothing but what is commonly right, namely that you satisfy the laws of Holy Church and release those men of God you have imprisoned and that you receive our Lord Stephen, Archbishop of Canterbury, and all his fellow bishops who have sought exile abroad, back in peace to England.'

When the king heard this his face became angry. 'Let me now reveal my innermost thoughts to you; you wish to make me swear to return all things to the Church, and I will do what you wish, but as soon as that Stephen . . . enters my land I shall hang him. . . .'

The legates responded: 'We have come here to discover whether your cause is, as you assert, just and right; and if it seems to us that when your cause has been heard, you have neglected anything that you owe to your Lord the Pope and Holy Church and the clergy of England, you shall promptly make satisfaction to Holy Church by our judgment and decision and you will submit to any punishment which we impose upon you. But if, on the other hand, your cause is just as you believe, then we shall relax the Interdict on England.'

The king answered the legates, 'Judge well, for I know that my Lord Pope is my spiritual father and that he is the vicar of the Blessed Peter and that I ought to obey him in spiritual matters; but in earthly concerns, which are part of my domain, I shall never obey him. . . .'

Finally, the king proposed the following solution. 'Because of my love for the Lord Pope, I offer that Master Stephen Langton resign the office of Archbishop and the Lord Pope may choose whomever he wills to be Archbishop and I shall receive him. . . .' But Pandulf could not accept: 'Holy Church can never depose an Archbishop without due cause.'

In full in *Annales Monastici* (see p. 140), i, pp. 211–15.

Letter of Innocent III to King John, 27 February 1213

To John, illustrious King of the English, a spirit of sounder understanding.

... You have offered to make restitution on those terms which we had had conveyed to you by our beloved sons and members of our household Pandulf the subdeacon and brother Durand. But because it was your fault that peace was not restored on those terms and because you have since attempted worse outrages than before, we are no longer bound to terms which were, in the main, conciliatory, for you have shown yourself unworthy of conciliation. But that we may overcome evil with good and deprive you of all ground of excuse, we are still ready to accept those terms if before the 1st of June next ensuing, on the oaths of four of your barons, swearing on your soul in your presence and at your command, and by your own letters patent you renew your promise, faithfully and effectively to implement those terms according to the interpretations and explanations we have thought fit to append for the removal of every shade of misunderstanding, and if within this time limit you have by your letters patent made all this known to our venerable brother Stephen Archbishop of Canterbury and to his bishops who are with him. Otherwise, by the example of him who with a strong hand freed his people from the bondage of Pharaoh, we intend with a mighty arm to free the English Church from your bondage. ...

The terms with which we charged our aforenamed envoys, we send to you enclosed in the present letter. The interpretations and explanations are as follows:

First, in the presence of our legate or delegate you will solemnly and unreservedly swear to abide by our commands, in respect of all matters for which you are excommunicated by us, and you will grant genuine peace and a full guarantee to our venerable brethren Stephen Archbishop of Canterbury, William Bishop of London, Eustace, Bishop of Ely, Giles, Bishop of Hereford, Jocelyn, Bishop of Bath and Hugh, Bishop of Lincoln, and to our beloved sons the prior and monks of Canterbury, and to Robert FitzWalter and Eustace de Vesci, and to all others, clerical and lay, concerned in this business. At the same time you will publicly take an oath in the presence of our legate or delegate that you will not injure the said individuals . . . and will forgo all your anger against them and receive them into your favour and in good faith maintain them there and that you will not hinder the said archbishop and bishops, nor cause or permit them to be hindered from freely exercising their office. . . . On these matters you will give both to us and to the archbishop and to the individual bishops your own letters patent and you will cause your bishops, earls and barons . . . to give oaths and letters patent that they will work in good faith to ensure that this agreement be firmly kept; and, that if you contravene it (which God forbid!) either personally or through agents, they will stand fast by the apostolic commands on the Church's side against the violators of the guarantee and the peace and you will forever lose the custody of vacant churches. . . . If you so wish the Archbishop and bishops will give you, saving the honour of God and the Church, a sworn and written guarantee that they will not either personally or by agents attempt anything against your person or your crown, provided you retain inviolate the said guarantee and peace. You will make full restitution of things seized and pay adequate compensation for losses to all clergy and all laymen concerned in this business—not only in respect of chattels but also of liberties, and those liberties when restored you will maintain. . . .

You will immediately cause all clergy whom you detain to be unconditionally released and restored to their personal liberty, and similarly all laymen who are detained because of this business. Promptly on the arrival of him who is to absolve you, you will arrange for 8,000 pounds of legal sterling, as restitution of seized property, to be assigned to the envoys of the archbishop and bishops and monks of Canterbury for the paying of debts and the meeting of expenses . . . to the Archbishop of Canterbury 2,500 pounds, to the Bishop of London 750 pounds, to the Bishop of Ely 1,500 pounds, to the Bishop of Hereford 750 pounds . . . to the prior and monks of Canterbury 1,000 pounds. . . . That ban also, commonly termed outlawry, which you had issued against ecclesiastics, you will publicly withdraw. . . . You will moreover revoke the ban of outlawry on laymen concerned in this business, and you will remit the homage which after the Interdict you took from the tenants of churches contrary to the custom of the realm and to ecclesiastical liberty. If any question of fact arise touching the losses . . . let the matter be publicly settled by our delegate or legate on proof received. When all these conditions have been duly fulfilled, the sentence of Interdict will be relaxed.

The Lateran the 27th of February in the sixteenth year of our Pontificate.

In full and translated in *Selected Letters of Innocent III* (**10**), pp. 130–6.

document 13

The Waverley Annals' description of John under year 1214

In this year there arose great discord between the King of England and his barons, the latter demanding from him the laws of St Edward and the liberties granted by later kings. For in the time of his father and during most of his own reign, custom became too much corrupted and changed; for he tried certain men without the justice of their pleas, and condemned others to a violent death; instead of laws he has raised up the tyranny of his will. Since the king denied these charges and refused to give way, a large group of magnates joined together to oppose him.

In full in *Annales Monastici* (see p. 140), ii, p. 282.

document 14

Wendover's account of the meetings at St Paul's 1213 and Bury St Edmunds, 1214

In the same year on the 8 September at St Paul's in London, Stephen Langton met the bishops, abbots and barons of the realm . . . and at this meeting there is a rumour that the said

archbishop called together certain important princes and began
to address them secretly as follows: 'You have heard that when
I absolved the king at Winchester I compelled him to swear an
oath to destroy all evil customs and revive all good laws, namely
the laws of King Edward. Now we have found a certain Charter
of King Henry I through which, if you wish it, you can recover
those liberties which you have long since lost.' He then showed
them the Charter of Henry I and had it read aloud to them. . . .

A further meeting was called in the following year at Bury
St Edmunds where the earls and barons met for discussion.
When they had formerly conspired against the king, a Charter
of Henry I had been produced in their midst by Stephen
Langton, Archbishop of Canterbury; now this Charter contained liberties and laws of St Edward, the King of England,
granted alike to the Church of England and the barons of the
Realm, and also certain liberties which Henry I himself had
added. Therefore they met at the Church of St Edmund, king
and martyr, and swore above the High Altar that if King John
refused to grant their said laws and liberties, then they would
make war on him, and break off their fealty, until he would
confirm their demands by a Charter under his seal. And at
length they all agreed, that they would meet the king after
Christmas and persuade him to grant their liberties, and in the
meantime they would provide themselves with horses and arms
so that if the king refused their demands they could capture his
castles and compel him to give them full satisfaction.

In full in Wendover, *Flores Historiarum* (see p. 140), pp. 263–4, 293–4.

John's Charter to the Church 1214

John, by the grace of God, King of England, Lord of Ireland,
Duke of Normandy and Aquitaine, Count of Anjou, to archbishops, bishops, earls, barons, knights, bailiffs and all who will
see or hear of this letter, greeting. Know that . . . we wish to
make full satisfaction to our bishops for the losses suffered in

the time of the Interdict and also to make provision in perpetuity for the whole Church in England: namely that, whatever custom of our own time or of our predecessors has been observed so far in the Church and whatever rights we have claimed so far in the election of any prelates, we now freely . . . and with the common consent of our barons, grant and by this Charter confirm that each and every church and monastery, cathedral and conventual, shall be allowed free election in perpetuity, of prelates both great and small; saving to us and our heirs the custody of churches and monasteries during vacancies, as is our right. Moreover, we promise not to hinder this freedom or prevent through our servants the freedom of election to choose their own pastors, whenever they wish, once the see becomes vacant, although the licence to elect must first be sought from us or our heirs, a licence which we promise not to deny or delay. And if by chance the licence is delayed, the electors may proceed to canonically elect their candidate. Further, after the celebration of the election our agreement is required, but we promise not to delay that unless there is some good reason why we ought not to agree. . . .

In Latin in *Stubbs' Charters* (**13**), pp. 283-4.

document 16
The king's letter to the pope, 29 May 1215

From the King to the Pope greeting. . . . We thank Your Holiness for the many letters which you sent on our behalf to the Lord Archbishop of Canterbury and his suffragan bishops, and to the magnates and barons of the realm. You should know that the barons have paid no heed to your letters and that the archbishop and his suffragans have failed to carry out your commands. We, however, listened to your commands and handed over our land to be held of the Patrimony of St Peter, the Blessed Church, and your Holiness. Moreover, we took the Cross and sought the benefit and privilege of crusaders, that our lands be not disturbed or affected by the evil customs which we proposed to cover the expenses of our journey to the Holy Land.

After we took the Cross, and wished to proceed with humility in all our actions, for the sake of our good name, we offered our barons that we would discuss all evil customs and abolish all those introduced in our own times, as well as those introduced in the time of our brother, King Richard. Further any evil custom introduced in the time of our father we would discuss with the counsel of our tenants. But none of this satisfied our barons; they rejected all our offers.

On realising, therefore, that they were clearly threatening to disturb the peace of our realm, we asked the Lord Archbishop of Canterbury and his suffragans that they should impose your mandate on the barons, namely that they should perform the customary service according to your letters. Afterwards, if any, who had a grievance, should wish to petition us, they should do so with humility and without arms. We also asked that they should excommunicate any who, after these offers, should disturb the peace of the Realm, and it seemed to the Bishop of Exeter and Master Pandulf, who were also present, that excommunication was the correct sentence for this crime.

But the Archbishop of Canterbury replied that he could not impose this sentence because he knew your view on the matter. It seemed to us that he ought to have excommunicated them since we had commanded a large troop of foreign mercenaries to come to our aid. The Archbishop promised that if we would send them back, he would not only excommunicate any offenders, but he would also resist them as much as he could. So we sent our mercenaries back.

Afterwards we offered them, through our letters patent and through the archbishop and two or three bishops chosen by them, that we should choose four men and that they should choose four, to meet under your guidance to settle all quarrels, and that you should have the casting vote. So, although they have been unwilling to humble themselves to us as they should, we have, for the service of God and the relief of the Holy Land, humbled ourselves, as we have said, before them. And then we even offered them full justice by the judgment of their peers; but this they also refused. . . .

133

Therefore, Blessed Father, we have brought these matters to your notice so that, according to your custom, you may see what has happened to us and decide what you think.

In Latin in Rymer, *Foedera* (see p. 141), pp. 66-7.

document 17
Ralph of Coggeshall lists the royal barons in May 1215

And now throughout the length and breadth of the land, once the royal capital had been seen to be taken, all the magnates joined the Army of God. The exceptions were the Earls of Warenne, Arundel, Chester, Pembroke, Ferrars and Salisbury, and a few barons like William Briwerre and a few others; yet even these men saw their knights and vassals go over to the baronial camp.

Ralph of Coggeshall (see p. 140), p. 171.

document 18
Wendover lists the rebel barons meeting at Stamford, Easter 1215

Robert FitzWalter, Eustace de Vesci, Richard de Percy, Robert de Ros, Peter de Brus, Nicholas de Stuteville, Saer Earl of Winchester, R. Earl of Clare, H. Earl of Clare, Roger Earl of Bigod, William de Mowbray, Roger de Cressy, Ranulf Fitz-Robert, Robert de Ver, Fulk FitzWarin, William Malet, William of Monteacuto, William of Bellocampo, Simon de Kyme, William Marshall Junior, William Maudit, Roger de Montbegon, John FitzRobert, John FitzAlan, Geoffrey de Laval, Osbert FitzAlan, William de Hobregge, Osbert de Vallibus, Geoffrey de Gant, Maurice de Gant, Richard of Brackley, Richard de Muntfichet, William de Lanvallei, Geoffrey de Mandeville, Earl of Essex, and William his brother, William of Huntingfield, Robert of Greslei, Geoffrey Constable of Meautun, Alexander de Pointon, Peter FitzJohn, Alexander of Sutuna, Osbert de Bobi, John Constable of Chester, Thomas of Mulutun, and many others. All these men conspired against the king with Stephen, Archbishop of Canterbury, as their leader.

Wendover, *Flores Historiarum* (see p. 140), pp. 297–8.

(see p. 140)

The Twenty-Five of Magna Carta

document 19

Richard Earl of Clare, William de Fors Count of Aumale, Geoffrey de Mandeville Earl of Gloucester, Saer de Quenci Earl of Winchester, Henry de Bohun Earl of Hereford, Roger Bigod Earl of Norfolk, Robert de Vere Earl of Oxford, William Marshal junior, Robert FitzWalter, Gilbert de Clare, Eustace de Vesci, Hugh Bigod, William de Mowbray the Mayor of London, William de Lanvallei, Robert de Ros, John de Lacy constable of Chester, Richard de Percy, John FitzRobert, William Malet, Geoffrey de Sai, Roger de Montbegon, William of Huntingfield, Richard de Muntfichet and William de Albini of Belvoir.

Holt (24), Appendix v, p. 338.

Extracts from 'Magna Carta'

document 20

1. . . . In the first place have granted to God and by this our present charter confirmed, for us and our heirs in perpetuity, that the English church shall be free and have its rights undiminished and its liberties unimpaired. . . . We have also granted to all the free men of our realm for ourselves and our heirs for ever, all the liberties written below, to have and to hold, them and their heirs, from us and our heirs.

135

2. If any of our earls or barons, or others holding of us in chief by knight service shall die, and at his death his heir be of full age and owe relief, he shall have his inheritance on payment of the ancient relief, namely the heir or heirs of an earl £100 for a whole earl's barony, the heir or heirs of a baron £100 for a whole barony, the heir or heirs of a knight 100s at most for a whole knight's fee; and anyone who owes less shall give less according to the ancient usage of fiefs.

3. If, however, the heir of any such person has been under age and in wardship, when he comes of age he shall have his inheritance without relief or fine.

4. The guardian of the land of such an heir who is under age shall not take from the land more than the reasonable revenues, customary dues and services, and that without destruction and waste of men or goods. . . .

8. No widow shall be compelled to marry so long as she wishes to live without a husband, provided she gives security that she will not marry without our consent if she holds of us, or without the consent of the lord of whom she holds, if she holds of another. . . .

12. No scutage or aid is to be levied in our realm except by the common consent of our realm, unless it is for the ransom of our person, the knighting of our eldest son, or the first marriage of our eldest daughter; and for these only a reasonable aid is to be levied. . . .

13. And the city of London is to have all its ancient liberties and free customs both by land and water. Furthermore we will grant that all other cities, boroughs, towns and ports shall have all their liberties and free customs . . .

16. No man shall be compelled to perform more service for a knight's fee than is due therefrom, or from any other free tenement.

17. Common pleas shall not follow our court but shall be held in some fixed place . . .

24. No sheriff, constable, coroner or other of our bailiffs may hold pleas of the Crown.

25. All shires, hundreds, wapentakes and ridings shall be at the ancient farm without any increment, except in our demesne manors . . .

34. The writ called 'praecipe' shall not in future be issued to anyone in respect of any holding whereby a free man may lose his court . . .

36. Henceforth nothing shall be given or taken from the writ of inquisition of life or limb, but is shall be given freely and not refused . . .

39. No free man shall be taken or imprisoned, or disseised or outlawed or exiled or in any way ruined, nor will we go or send against him, except by the lawful judgment of his peers or by the law of the land.

40. To no one will we sell, to no one will we deny or delay right or justice . . .

45. We will not make justices, constables, sheriffs or bailiffs who do not know the law of the land and mean to observe it well . . .

48. All evil customs of forests and warrens, foresters and warreners, sheriffs and their servants, river banks and their wardens are to be investigated at once in every county by twelve sworn knights of the same county who are to be chosen by working men of the county, and within forty days of the enquiry they are to be abolished by them beyond recall, provided that we . . . know of it first.

49. We will restore at once all hostages and charters delivered to us by Englishmen as securities for peace or faithful service.

50. We will dismiss completely from their offices the relations of Gerard D'Athée that henceforth they shall have no office in England, Englelard de Cigogné, Peter and Guy and Andrew de Chanceux . . . and all their followers . . .

52. If any one has been disseised or deprived by us without lawful judgment of his pleas, of lands, castles, liberties or his rights we will restore them to him at once . . .

58. We will restore at once the son of Llywelyn and all the hostages from Wales and all the charters delivered to us as security for peace . . .

61. Since, moreover, we have granted the aforesaid things for God, for the reform of our realm and the better settling of the quarrel which has arisen between us and our barons, and since we wish these things to be enjoyed fully and undisturbed, we give and grant them the following security;

namely, that the barons shall choose any Twenty-Five barons of the realm they wish, who with all their right are to observe and maintain . . . the peace and liberties which we have granted and confirmed to them by this our present charter; so that if we . . . offend against anyone in any way or transgress any of the articles of peace, and the offence is indicated to four of the aforesaid twenty-five barons, those four barons shall come to us . . . and bring it to our notice and ask that we have it redressed without delay. And if we . . . do not redress the offence within forty days from the time when it was brought to our notice . . . the aforesaid four barons should refer the case to the rest of the twenty-five and these twenty-five with the commune of the whole land shall distress and distrain us in every way they can, namely by seizing our castles, lands and possessions . . . until in their judgment, amends have been made.

In full and translated in Holt (**24**), pp. 317–37, where it is compared, clause by clause, with the 'Articles of the Barons' and the Reissue of 1225.

Bibliography

PRIMARY SOURCES

Throughout the Angevin period the historian has to rely basically on three types of literary evidence: the work of chroniclers and annalists, the letters and official records of governmental activity, English, French and papal, and several contemporary descriptive accounts like the *Dialogue of the Exchequer* (**28**). Although usually the least reliable, the monastic chronicler remains the most fascinating source; as Powicke has said, 'The Medieval Chronicle remains too essentially incomplete to be accurate, yet it is so near the heart of things, is the result of so many influences, that it is essentially true' (**99**). The monks collected and compiled material for a wide variety of events of local, national and European significance, the material usually being written up by one monk at the end of the year. Thus the chronology was usually accurate and some continuity was maintained. The material was sometimes sifted and improvements made in the text over erasures as new evidence came to light. Although, therefore, this may have been scissors and paste history as Galbraith has pointed out (**19**), it did have honesty of purpose: 'If it please any man to amend this tale', wrote one monk, 'I give him leave. But let him see to it that he alters none of the facts . . . for I call truth herself to witness that I write nothing . . . save what is found recorded in the writings of old time or heard from the lips of ancient or faithful witnesses.' The weakness of the medieval chronicler lay usually in his bias, centred around local and ecclesiastical events, and his complete lack of historical understanding: he rarely criticised his sources, explained causation or showed any sense of the unity of historical development. On the other hand the historian must be grateful for the often copious, sometimes lively, portrayal of contemporary events.

The main chronicles for John's reign appear in Latin in the following editions:

Roger Wendover, *Chronica*, ed. H. O. Coxe, English Historical Society, 1841–4. This includes the 'Flores Historiarum'.

Matthew Paris, *Chronica Majora*, ed. H. R. Luard, Rolls Series, 1872–83.

Walter of Coventry, *Memoriale*, ed. W. Stubbs, Rolls Series, 1872–3.

Ralph of Coggeshall, *Chronicon Anglicanum*, ed. J. Stevenson, Rolls Series, 1875.

Histoire des ducs de Normandie, ed. F. Michel, Soc. de l'Histoire de France, 1840.

In addition to the main chroniclers, the accounts of the monastic annalists have been printed in:

Annales Monastici, ed. H. R. Luard, Rolls Series, 1864–6.

Roger Wendover was recalled to the great Benedictine monastery at St Albans in 1219 after failing to administer the small daughter house at Belvoir; thereafter he remained in the library at St Albans, an important geographical site, until his death in 1236, and compiled the chronicle which was to be responsible for the legend of 'Bad King John'. The importance of Wendover's chronicle is its detail; much of this is irrelevant and inaccurate since the author wanted a good dramatic story, but he does provide much material that is not available elsewhere. Unfortunately the source is very unreliable: he confused the original Magna Carta with the reissue of 1225, made no attempt to check such sources as papal letters for their authenticity and accuracy, and recorded very confused accounts of the critical years 1213–15. Such stories as the capture of Mons Alba in 1206, the William de Braose affair [**doc. 6**] and the August night in 1212 when John received letters warning him against a Welsh invasion are contrived, overdramatic and of little historical value. Walter of Coventry, although less copious, is a much more reliable source than Wendover. He was an Austin Canon writing about 1227, a strong patriot with a fair sense of justice: where Wendover attributed the loss of Normandy to John's weakness, Coventry pointed out that John was not helped by the unreliable Norman barons. In 1215, too, he made both parties equally responsible for the struggle and blamed the barons for the start of the civil war, even though John captured Rochester first. Moreover, when in doubt about the authenticity of an event, Coventry used *ut dicitur* or *sine certo auctore*, a definite advance on Wendover's technique.

Coventry was perceptive too: he noted the purpose of the expedition to Poitou in 1206, the recovery of the lost lands in Normandy, and also saw the point of John's surrender to the pope in 1213, to get papal support against the barons and Philip Augustus.

Ralph of Coggeshall, a Cistercian abbot, is particularly valuable for European news, such as crusading, and local events, like the death in 1206 of the Bishop of Lincoln. His account is brief and particularly prejudiced against the king, the 'oppressor' of the Cistercians who refused to allow Cistercian abbots to attend the general Chapter at Citeaux in France. Under the year 1213, however, he does attempt to weigh up the reasons for the baronial refusal of scutage, and his account of the Bouvines campaign in the following year attempts to explain John's failure. Apart from these few patches the *Chronicle* is merely a list of events.

Finally, the *Histoire des ducs* though difficult to get hold of, is a reliable and full account of the events of the reign, particularly with regard to the Angevin empire, while the *Annales* provide much of the basic material for the copyists of the Chronicles and also give much that is of local value. The Margam Annalist, for instance, is the only English record of the connection of William de Braose and the death of Arthur.

To corroborate the accuracy of the chroniclers the historian must use the official records, the letters and charters of the king's chancery and the records of judicial and financial proceedings in the king's court. These are particularly full for John's reign since in 1200 he ordered the first regular enrolment of all chancery letters. In addition, of course, we have similar material from Philip Augustus's government, though less full, and the papal government, even fuller than John's. The main sources of such material are:

Rotuli Litterarum Clausarum, ed. T. D. Hardy, Record Commission, 1833–4.
Rotuli Litterarum Patentium, ed. T. D. Hardy, Record Commission, 1835.
Foedera, ed. T. Rymer, Record Commission, 1816–30; reprinted Gregg Press, 1967.
Selected letters of Pope Innocent III concerning England, ed. C. R. Cheney and W. H. Semple, Nelson, 1963.
Pleas before the King or his Justices, ed. D. M. Stenton, Selden Society, 1948–9.

The Memoranda Roll I John, ed. H. G. Richardson, Pipe Roll Society, 1943.

The Prest Rolls, ed. J. C. Holt, Pipe Roll Society, 1961.

The Curia Regis Rolls, ed. C. T. Flower, Selden Society, 1942.

And, of course, the various Pipe Rolls, published by the Pipe Roll Society, most of them under the editorship of Lady Stenton.

The Chancery Rolls, although a new and particularly valuable source for John's reign, are certainly not complete: there are none at all for 1209–12 and no close rolls for 1208–9. Further, each roll contains gaps and omissions that it is difficult to fill, so that we have no evidence, for instance, about the early years of the Interdict. This gap is partly filled, however, by spasmodic household records like the Mise Rolls, recording the king's personal expenditure, and the Prest Rolls, the payments made to Household officials. The Pipe Rolls are complete for John's reign, except for two gaps in 1213 and 1215 and the Memoranda Rolls are a very useful source of evidence for John's financial relations with his barons. The records of judicial proceedings, however, copied down by a clerk in the court are seldom complete and, since they were used solely to enable a judge to continue after an adjournment, they rarely contained records of judgments. Again this can be partially rectified by feet of fines. Finally, the records and letters of the French and papal chanceries have particularly important bearing on English affairs, especially during the interdict and the events of 1215–16. Professor Knowles used papal archives extensively, for instance, in his reconstruction of the proceedings at Canterbury in 1205–6 (**94**).

SECONDARY SOURCES

1 Barlow, F. *The Feudal Kingdom of England*, Longmans, 1955.

2 Barrow, G. W. S. *Feudal Britain*, Edward Arnold, 1956.

3 Barnes, P. M. Introduction to *Pipe Roll 14 John*, Pipe Roll Society, new series vol. 30, 1954.

4 Barnes, P. M. Introduction to *Pipe Roll 14 John*, Pipe Roll Society, new series vol. 35, 1959.

5 Brookes, F. W. *English Naval Forces*, Pordes, 1962.

6 Cartellieri, A. *Philip II August*, Leipzig, 1900.

7 Chaytor, H. J. *Savaric de Mauleon, Baron and Troubadour*, Cambridge University Press, 1939.

8   Cheney, C. R. *From Becket to Langton*, Manchester University Press, 1956.
9   Cheney, C. R. *Hubert Walter*, Nelson, 1967.
10 Cheney, C. R. and Semple, W. H. *Selected letters of Pope Innocent III to England*, Nelson, 1953.
11 Croslan, J. *William the Marshal*, Peter Owen, 1962.
12 Davis, H. W. C. *England under the Normans and Angevins*, 13th edn, Methuen, 1949.
13 Davis, H. W. C. *Stubbs' Select Charters*, 9th edn, Oxford University Press, 1913.
14 Davis, R. H. C. *King Stephen*, Longman, 1967.
15 Douglas, D. C. *English Historical Documents*, vol. ii, Eyre & Spottiswoode, 1953.
16 Flower, C. T. Introduction to the *Curia Regis Rolls*, Selden Society, vol. 42, 1943.
17 Galbraith, V. H. *Roger Wendover and Mathew Paris*, Glasgow, 1944.
18 Galbraith, V. H. *Studies in the Public Records*, London, 1948.
19 Galbraith, V. H. *Historical Research in Medieval England*, Athlone Press, 1951.
20 Hollister, W. *Anglo Saxon Military Institutions*, Oxford University Press, 1962.
21 Hollister, W. *Military Organization of Norman England*, Oxford University Press, 1965.
22 Holt, J. C. Introduction to the *Praestita Rolls*, Pipe Roll Society, 1961.
23 Holt, J. C. *The Northerners*, Oxford University Press, 1961.
24 Holt, J. C. *Magna Carta*, Cambridge University Press, 1965.
25 Howells, M. *Regalian Rights*, Athlone Press, 1962.
26 Hoyt, R. W. *The Royal Demesne*, Oxford University Press, 1950.
27 Jennings, I. *Magna Carta: its influence on the world today*, H.M.S.O., 1965.
28 Johnson, C. *Dialogue of the Exchequer*, Nelson, 1950.
29 Jolliffe, J. E. A. *Angevin Kingship*, 2nd edn, Black, 1963.
30 Lawrence, C. H. ed., *The English Church and the Papacy in the Middle Ages*, Burns & Oates, 1963.
31 Lloyd, J. E. *History of Wales*, Longmans, 3rd edn, 1939.
32 McKechnie, W. S. *Magna Carta*, 2nd edn, Glasgow, 1914.
33 Maitland, F. W. *Constitutional History of England*, Cambridge University Press, 1908.

34 Mitchell, S. K. *Studies in Taxation under John and Henry III*, Yale University Press, 1914.

35 Norgate, K. *John Lackland*, Macmillan, 1902.

36 Otway-Ruthven, A. J. *A History of Medieval Ireland*, Benn, 1968.

37 Painter, S. *The Reign of King John*, John Hopkins Press, 1949.

38 Painter, S. *Studies in the History of the English Feudal Baronage*, Baltimore, 1943.

39 Plucknett, T. F. T. *Concise History of the Common Law*, 5th edn, Butterworths, 1956.

40 Pollock, F. and Maitland, F. W. *A History of English Law*, Cambridge University Press, 1898.

41 Poole, A. L. *From Domesday Book to Magna Carta*, 2nd edn, Oxford University Press, 1955.

42 Poole, A. L. *Obligations of Society in the Twelfth and Thirteenth Centuries*, Oxford University Press, 1946.

43 Poole, R. L. *The Exchequer in the Twelfth Century*, Oxford University Press, 1912.

44 Post, G. *Studies in Medieval Legal Thought*, Princeton University Press, 1964.

45 Powicke, F. M., in *Cambridge Medieval History*, vol. vi, chapter 7, Cambridge University Press, 1929.

46 Powicke, F. M. *The Loss of Normandy*, 2nd edn, Manchester University Press, 1961.

47 Powicke, F. M. *Stephen Langton*, Oxford University Press, 1927.

48 Powicke, M. *Military Obligation in Medieval England*, Oxford University Press, 1965.

49 Ramsey, J. H. *The Angevin Empire*, Macmillan, 1903.

50 Richardson, H. G. and Sayles, G. O. *The Governance of Medieval England*, Edinburgh University Press, 1963.

51 Richardson, H. G., Introduction to the *Memoranda Roll I John*, Pipe Roll Society, 59, 1943.

52 Richardson, H. G. *The Administration of Ireland*, Irish Manuscripts Commission, 1963.

53 Roth, C. *The History of the Jews in England*, 3rd edn, Oxford University Press, 1964.

54 Sayles, G. O. *The Medieval Foundations of England*, Methuen, 1948.

55 Smith, S. Introduction to *Pipe Roll 7 John*, Pipe Roll Society, 19, 1941.

56 Stenton, D. M. Introductions to *Pipe Rolls 1–6, 8, 10, 11, 13 John*, Pipe Roll Society, 1935–53.

57 Stenton, D. M. Introduction to *Earliest Lincolnshire Assize Rolls*, Lincoln Record Society, 1926.

58 Stenton, D. M. Introduction to *Earliest Northampton Assize Rolls*, Northampton Record Society, 1930.

59 Stenton, D. M. Introduction to *Pleas before the King or his Justices*, Selden Society, 67, 1948.

60 Stenton, D. M. *English Justice between the Norman Conquest and the Great Charter*, Allen & Unwin, 1963.

61 Stenton, F. *The First Century of English Feudalism*, Oxford University Press, 1961.

62 Stubbs, W. *Constitutional History of England*, 3rd edn, Oxford University Press, 1883.

63 Thompson, F. *The First Century of Magna Carta*, Minnesota, 1925.

64 Thompson, F. *Magna Carta: its role in the making of the English Constitution*, Oxford University Press, 1948.

65 Tout, T. F. *Chapters in the Administrative History of Medieval England*, Manchester, 1920.

66 Ullman, W. *Principles of Government and Politics in the Middle Ages*, Methuen, 1961.

67 Warren, W. L. *King John*, Eyre & Spottiswoode, 1961.

68 West, F. W. *The Justiciarship in England*, Cambridge University Press, 1966.

ARTICLES, ESSAYS, AND PAMPHLETS

69 Adams, G. B. 'Innocent III and the Great Charter', in *Magna Carta Commemoration Essays*, Royal Historical Society, 1917.

70 Brooks, F. W. 'William de Wrotham and the office of Keeper of the King's Ports and Galleys', *English Historical Review*, xl, 1925.

71 Brown, R. A. 'The Treasury in the later twelfth century', in *Jenkinson Studies*, 1957.

72 Brown, R. A. 'Royal castle building in England', *English Historical Review*, lxx, 1955.

73 Cheney, C. R. 'The 25 of Magna Carta', *Bulletin of the John Rylands Library*, l, 1968.

145

74   Cheney, C. R. 'The alleged deposition of King John', in *Studies in Medieval History presented to F. M. Powicke*, Oxford University Press, 1948.

75   Cheney, C. R. 'King John and the papal interdict', *Bulletin of the John Rylands Library*, xxxi, 1948.

76   Cheney, C. R. 'King John's reaction to the interdict', *Transactions of the Royal Historical Society*, 4th ser., xxxi, 1949.

77   Cheney, C. R. 'The eve of Magna Carta', *Bulletin of the John Rylands Library*, xxxviii, 1956.

78   Cheney, C. R. 'The Church and Magna Carta', *Theology*, lxviii, June 1965.

79   Cheney, Mrs. M. 'The compromise of Arvanches', *English Historical Review*, 56, 1941.

80   Dickinson, J. C. *The Great Charter*, Historical Association Pamphlet, 1955.

81   Galbraith, V. H. 'A draft of Magna Carta', *Proceedings of the British Academy*, liii, 1967.

82   Harris, B. E. 'King John and the sheriffs' farms', *English Historical Review*, lxxix, 1964.

83   Holt, J. C. 'Philip Mark', *Transactions of the Thoroton Society*, lvi, 1952.

84   Holt, J. C. 'The barons and the Great Charter', *English Historical Review*, lxx, 1955.

85   Holt, J. C. 'The making of Magna Carta', *English Historical Review*, lxxii, 1957.

86   Holt, J. C. 'Rights and liberties in Magna Carta', in *Album Helen Maud Cam*, Louvain, 1960.

87   Holt, J. C. 'The St Albans Chroniclers and Magna Carta', *Transactions of the Royal Historical Society*, 5th ser., xiv, 1964.

88   Holt, J. C. *King John*, Historical Association Pamphlet, 1963.

89   Hurnard, N. D. 'The Jury of Presentment', *English Historical Review*, lvi, 1941.

90   Hurnard, N. D. 'Magna Carta, Clause 34', in *Studies in Medieval History presented to F. M. Powicke*, Oxford University Press, 1948.

91   Jenkinson, H. 'Financial Records of the Reign of King John', in *Magna Carta Commemoration Essays*, Royal Historical Society, 1917.

92   Jenks, E. 'The myth of Magna Carta', *Independent Review*, iv, 1904.

93   Jolliffe, J. E. A. 'The Chamber and castle treasures' in *Studies in Medieval History presented to F. M. Powicke*, Oxford University Press, 1948.

94   Knowles, D. 'The Canterbury Election', *English Historical Review*, liii, 1938.

95   Lyon, B. 'The money fief under the English kings', *English Historical Review*, lxvi, 1951.

96   McKechnie, W. S. 'Magna Carta 1215–1915', in *Magna Carta Commemoration Essays*, Royal Historical Society, 1917.

97   Mills, M. M. 'Experiments in Exchequer Procedure', *Transactions of the Royal Historical Society*, 4th ser., viii, 1925.

98   Powell, W. R. 'The administration of the Navy', *English Historical Review*, lxxi, 1956.

99   Powicke, F. M. 'Roger of Wendover and the Coggeshall Chronicle', *English Historical Review*, xxi, 1906.

100   Powicke, F. M. 'Per Judicium Parium', in *Magna Carta Commemoration Essays*, Royal Historical Society, 1917.

101   Powicke, F. M. 'The Bull "Miramur Plurimum"', *English Historical Review*, xliv, 1929.

102   Prestwich, J. O. 'War and finance in the Anglo Norman state', *Transactions of the Royal Historical Society*, 5th ser., iv, 1954.

103   Richardson, H. G. 'William of Ely', *Transactions of the Royal Historical Society*, 4th ser., xv, 1932.

104   Richardson, H. G. 'The morrow of the Great Charter', *Bulletin of the John Rylands Library*, xxviii, 1944.

105   Richardson, H. G. 'The morrow of the Great Charter, an addendum', *Bulletin of the John Rylands Library*, xxix, 1945.

106   Round, J. H. 'An unknown Charter of Liberties', *English Historical Review*, viii, 1893.

107   Sayles, G. O. *The Court of the King's Bench in Law and History*, Selden Society Lecture, 1959.

108   Stenton, D. M. 'King John and the Courts of Justice', *Proceedings of the British Academy*, xliv, 1958.

Index

Index

Triplex Forma Pacis, 51, 96
Tusculum, Cardinal Nicholas of, 43

Unknown Charter of Liberties, 47

Walter, Hubert, 5–6, 35, 62
Walter of Coventry, 140
Wakefield, Peter of, *see* Pontefract
Wendover, Roger of, 140

William de Braose, *see* de Braose
William de Mowbray, *see* de Mowbray
William de Warenne, *see* de Warenne
William, Bishop of Ely, 65, 69
William, Earl of Salisbury, *see* Salisbury
William the Lion, King of Scots, 27
Winchester, Saer de Quenci, Earl of, *see* de Quenci
Wrotham, William of, 61, 68

DATE DUE